# DRUNK DRIVING DEFENSE

Fifth Edition
2001 Cumulative Supplement

## LAWRENCE TAYLOR, J.D.
Long Beach, California

Member, California and Washington Bars
Former Deputy Public Defender, Los Angeles
Former Deputy District Attorney, Los Angeles
Former Fulbright Professor of Law, Osaka University

ASPEN LAW & BUSINESS
A Division of Aspen Publishers, Inc.
Gaithersburg     New York

This publication is designed to provide accurate and authoritative information in regard to the subject matter covered. It is sold with the understanding that the publisher is not engaged in rendering legal, accounting, or other professional services. If legal advice or other professional assistance is required, the services of a competent professional person should be sought.

— From a *Declaration of Principles* jointly adopted by
a Committee of the American Bar Association and a
Committee of Publishers and Associations

Permissions
Aspen Law & Business
1185 Avenue of the Americas
New York, NY 10036

Printed in the United States of America

1 2 3 4 5 6 7 8 9 0

Library of Congress Cataloging-in-Publication Data

Taylor, Lawrence, 1942-
    Drunk driving defense / Lawrence Taylor. — 5th ed.
        p.   cm.
    Includes bibliographical references and index.
    ISBN 0-7355-1146-2
    ISBN 0-7355-2245-6 (supplement)
    1. Drunk driving defense — United States.   2. Defense (Criminal procedure) —
United States.   I. Title.
KF2231.T39   1999
345.73'0247 — dc21                                                   99-41726
                                                                     CIP

*Fifth Edition*

# About Aspen Law & Business

Aspen Law & Business is a leading publisher of authoritative treatises, practice manuals, services, and journals for attorneys, corporate and bank directors, accountants, auditors, environmental compliance professionals, financial and tax advisors, and other business professionals. Our mission is to provide practical solution-based how-to information keyed to the latest original pronouncements, as well as the latest legislative, judicial, and regulatory developments.

We offer publications in the areas of accounting and auditing; antitrust; banking and finance; bankruptcy; business and commercial law; construction law; corporate law; criminal law; environmental compliance; government and administrative law; health law; insurance law; intellectual property; international law; legal practice and litigation; matrimonial and family law; pensions, benefits, and labor; real estate law; securities; and taxation.

Other Aspen Law & Business products treating criminal and litigation issues include:

**Almanac of the Federal Judiciary**
**Civil False Claims and Qui Tam Actions (Second Edition)**
**Civil RICO Practice Manual (Second Edition)**
**Department of Justice Manual (Second Edition)**
**Deposition Handbook (Third Edition)**
**Destruction of Evidence**
**Directory of Federal Court Guidelines**
**Discovery Practice (Third Edition)**
**Handbook of Connecticut Evidence (Third Edition)**
**Handbook of Illinois Evidence (Seventh Edition)**
**Handbook of Massachusetts Evidence (Seventh Edition)**
**Handbook of New York Evidence**
**Jury Selection (Second Edition)**
**The Law of Civil RICO**
**Mauet's Trial Notebook**
**Motion Practice (Third Edition)**
**The New Wigmore**
**New York Defender Digest**
**New York Evidence Handbook**
**Practice Under the Federal Sentencing Guidelines (Fourth Edition)**
**Tax Court Litigation**
**Wigmore on Evidence**

**ASPEN LAW & BUSINESS**
**A Division of Aspen Publishers, Inc.**
**A Wolters Kluwer Company**
*www.aspenpublishers.com*

## SUBSCRIPTION NOTICE

This Aspen Law & Business product is updated on a periodic basis with supplements to reflect important changes in the subject matter. If you purchased this product directly from Aspen Law & Business, we have already recorded your subscription for the update service.

If, however, you purchased this product from a bookstore and wish to receive future updates and revised or related volumes billed separately with a 30-day examination review, please contact our Customer Service Department at 1-800-234-1660, or send your name, company name (if applicable), address, and the title of the product to:

**ASPEN LAW & BUSINESS**
**A Division of Aspen Publishers, Inc.**
**7201 McKinney Circle**
**Frederick, MD 21704**

# CONTENTS

# II

## EVIDENCE

### 4.

### 5.

### 6.

Contents

# IV
_____

# TRIAL

## 13.
_____

# DRUNK DRIVING DEFENSE
## 2001 Cumulative Supplement

# I

## CRIME AND PUNISHMENT

# 1

## THE OFFENSE

### §1.3  Under the Influence of Alcohol

#### §1.3.1  Presumption of Intoxication from Blood-Alcohol Analysis

*Page 42.  Add at end of subsection:*

Counsel may encounter the increasingly prevalent situation where the prosecutor has filed drunk driving charges when the blood-alcohol level tested *below* the statutory level. The reasoning may be that, for example, the BAC was falling and that although tested an hour or two after the stop at .07 percent, retrograde extrapolation (see §5.2) indicates a probable level of .10 percent at the time of driving. This is, of course, speculation and quite susceptible to cross-examination. In addition, counsel may wish to consider an argument to the jury that, absent other compelling evidence, reasonable doubt *automatically* exists.

The logic is this: It appears that a rebuttable presumption exists when defendants are under the influence of alcohol at levels above, say, .08 percent — but not below that level. When the alcohol level is below .08 percent we can no longer predict with any confidence that the individual *is* impaired. However, there is not even a *rebuttable* presumption: the legislature in its infinite wisdom was not willing to give that edge to impairment versus non-impairment. Quite simply, the law makes the .05 to .08 percent zone a toss-up. Stated another way, absent other compelling evidence, it is just as possible that the person was not impaired as it is that he was . . . and 50–50 does not amount to proof "beyond a reasonable doubt."

This approach can be used in conjunction with an opening statement, suggested by attorney Paul Ahern of Minnetonka, Minnesota, in which he tells the jury that "Today, you will meet someone who knew when to say when — a person who tested under our state's legal limit, a person who knew when to stop drinking."

### §1.4    Over .08 or .10 Percent Blood Alcohol

*Page 43.  Add after carryover sentence:*

(Note: On October 23, 2000, President Clinton signed a new law requiring states to implement a 0.08 percent BAC standard as the legal level by 2004. Failure to do so would result in the loss of millions of dollars in federal highway funds.)

### §1.4.5    Admissibility of Non-Impairment Evidence

*Page 51.  Add new subsection after end of subsection 1.4.5:*

### §1.4.6    "Direct Breath" Statutes

### §1.4 Over .08 or .10 Percent Blood Alcohol

Many states have followed California in adopting so-called "direct breath" statutes in an attempt to avoid the scientific reality of variable partition ratios. (See §6.0.1 of the main volume for a discussion of partition ratio.)

The so-called "direct breath-alcohol" statute has come under considerable scientific fire. One world-renowned blood-alcohol expert, for example, has shown that implicit in such statutes is an equation that incorrectly describes the relationship between blood- and breath-alcohol concentration in a human subject. Simpson, *The New "Direct Breath" Statutes: Both Bad Law and Bad Science,* 6(4) DWI Journal 1 (1991). In another article, written by Simpson and Professor Dominick Labianca, the scientists concluded that the statutes "thus put into law the relationship, blood-alcohol concentration (BAC) equals breath-alcohol concentration (BrAC), which is incorrect." Labianca and Simpson, *Medicolegal Alcohol Determination: Variability of the Blood- to Breath-Alcohol Ratio and Its Effect on Reported Breath-Alcohol Concentrations,* 33 European Journal of Clinical Chemistry 919 (1995). The direct breath statute "is tantamount to instructing jurors that the defendant's blood/breath ratio was 2100:1 or greater, when he/she was tested, and that the defendant is not permitted to rebut this presumption in any way" — despite the widely accepted fact that partition ratios vary widely. *Supra* at 923.

## §1.5   Under the Influence of Drugs

### Page 57. Add at of section:

Any law enforcement officer who testifies to recognition of symptoms of specific drugs must, of course, be qualified to do so — and the simple fact is that very few are. Many have received no formal training of any kind; others rely on reading materials or field experience. The credentials of any officer claiming to be a drug recognition expert (DRE) should be investigated, and his expertise challenged in a foundational motion *in limine* or on voir dire of the witness.

In *State v. Baity,* 991 P.2d 1151 (2000), for example, the Washington Supreme Court held that under the *Frye* test a DRE must follow a complete 12-step protocol, as originally developed by the Los Angeles Police Department (see *supra*) and later refined into a standardized curriculum by the National Highway Traffic Safety Administration:

> To be certified as a DRE, an officer must complete a three-phase program of instruction. First, the officer must attend a 16-hour 'preschool,' which involves an overview of the DRE program, and instruction on the seven drug categories and basic drug terminology. Second, the officer must complete a 56-hour DRE school program. The program consists of 30 modules of instruction, including an overview of the development and validation of the drug evaluation process, and sessions on each drug category. Additionally, the officer must pass a written examination before beginning

the next phase of training. Finally, the officer begins certification training. Certification requires the officer participate in a minimum of 12 complete examinations under the supervision of a trained DRE instructor. Of those 12 evaluations, the officer must identify a minimum 75 percent toxicological corroboration rate. The officer must then pass another written examination and a separate skills demonstration examination performed in front of two DRE instructors before he or she becomes certified as a DRE. Finally, the officer must maintain an up-to-date resume or curriculum vitae.

Additionally, a DRE must be recertified every two years. During that time period, the DRE is required to conduct four hands-on evaluations and to attend eight hours of in-service training.

## §1.6   Felony Drunk Driving: DUI with Injury

### §1.6.3   Murder: DUI with Inferred Malice

*Page 67.  Add at end of second paragraph:*

See also *People v. Murray*, 275 Cal. Rptr. 498 (1990), where the prosecution offered evidence that the defendant had attended a drinking driver education program and had stated that he had learned a lot from it. This was held properly admitted to show awareness of the life-threatening risk of drunk driving — and therefore the existence of implied malice.

## §1.9   Affirmative Defenses

### §1.9.2   Duress

*Page 76.  Add at end of subsection:*

A California court has held that duress is not applicable to an administrative license suspension hearing — impliedly recognizing its application in a criminal prosecution. Appellant in that case testified that a guest at a party threatened him with a knife; when he tried to leave the party, the knife-wielding guest followed him outside and it became necessary to get in his car and flee. The argument was that the defenses of necessity and duress applied, as driving under the circumstances was necessary to avoid serious injury or death. The suspension was upheld by the hearing officer, but this was reversed by the superior court. The court of appeals reversed, apparently reasoning that duress is a defense that negates *intent,* and state of mind was not relevant to the administrative proceeding. In also dismissing necessity as a defense, the court apparently ruled that equitable principles simply do not apply to DMV hearings:

> Even in the absence of considerations involving duress as negating the element of intent, the relevant statutes and their clear public policy preclude the application of the necessity defense to administrative per se hearings. The relevant provisions plainly and fully involve a remedial scheme that does not leave room for the discretionary application of equittable defenses. . . .
>
> In contrast to a criminal prosecution for drunk driving, the administrative remedy involving the suspension of driver's licenses was designed to be a "swift and certain" method of deterring such conduct. . . . It would be inconsistent with the purpose of this fact-finding procedure, and with the intent to suspend the driving privilege of those who are thus found to have been driving under the influence, to rescind the suspension for reasons that have nothing to do with whether the person was in fact driving while intoxicated. *Foster v. Reed,* — Cal. App. 4th — (1999).

But see *Curtin v. DMV,* 123 Cal. App. 3d 481 (1981), where another California court applied equitable principles to the administrative hearing:

> It is undeniably true that under any reasonable concept, right and justice would be defeated by the erroneous suspension of [plaintiff's] driver's license. And it is a basic principle of jurisprudence, at least in the absence of some transcendent public interest, that *equity* will assert itself in those situations where right and justice would be defeated but for its intervention.

# 3

# THE ADMINISTRATIVE LICENSE SUSPENSION

## §3.0 Implied Consent

### §3.0.1 Double Jeopardy: Criminal and Administrative Punishment

*Page 113. Add before first paragraph:*

The Ninth Circuit of the U.S. Court of Appeals has applied the reasoning in *Hudson* to an Alaskan drunk driving case. In holding that a driver's license suspension did not bar subsequent criminal charges arising out of the same incident, the court listed the following reasons for finding that an administrative suspension was only a civil rather than a criminal sanction:

1. License suspensions do not involve an affirmative disability or restraint. A driver's license is a privilege granted by the state, so license revocation is the loss of a privilege. It is immaterial that loss of the ability to drive may severely impact some individuals.
2. License suspensions have not historically been regarded as punishment.
3. A side effect of the suspension scheme may be deterrence, but that does not make the scheme criminal rather than civil.
4. The remedial purpose of license revocation is to protect

the public and, in the case of chemical tests, to obtain reliable evidence of intoxication.

5. The length of the suspension in this case (90 days) was not excessive in relation to the remedial purpose.

*Rivera v. Pugh,* ___ F.3d ___ (9th Cir. 1999, #98–35900).

**Page 113. Add new subsection after first paragraph:**

### §3.0.2   Due Process and the Administrative License Suspension

As any experienced DUI attorney knows, the administrative license suspension represents all that is wrong with a legal system that increasingly chooses to ignore constitutional safeguards. Aside from the issue of double jeopardy (see §3.0.1), the rules and procedures established for contesting an ALS represent a steadily deteriorating standard of due process generally. This is certainly due in large measure to legislators anxious to please voters and to such pressure groups as Mothers Against Drunk Driving, but it is also caused by legally ignorant bureaucrats staffing the state's department of motor vehicles. It is counsel's job to educate these officials and, where they will not be educated, to seek redress in court for denial of due process at the administrative level.

The following material was presented by attorney Les Hulnick of Wichita, Kansas, at the National College for DUI Defense's 1999 Summer Session at Harvard Law School.* It should provide counsel with an excellent overview of due process issues commonly encountered in the course of representing a client in a license suspension hearing.

## I.  Introduction

One unifying characteristic of the civil component of DUI charge — the administrative hearing or implied consent hearing — across the country is that it is an unusual, hybrid procedure

---

*Reprinted with permission.

in which constitutional safegards often seem to be cast aside in the name of political expediency, efficiency, and public safety. For example, the hearing officer routinely functions as both the judge and prosecutor, time deadlines (for the Government) often seem to be fluid and unenforced, and the notion of discovery for the citizen frequently seems to be regarded as a mere annoyance. Constitutional protections, however, do apply to these proceedings and, as a result, challenges based on due process, fundamental fairness, and other constitutional concepts, may be successfully lodged. This is not to suggest that successful challenges to the procedures are frequent or common, but they are possible and can have a tremendous impact on a large number of accused persons.

This outline will set forth some of the basic concepts which may support a constitutional challenge to the proceedings and detail some of the areas in which the constitutionality of the administrative proceedings recently have been challenged. This is not intended to be an exhaustive review of all possible constitutional issues inherent in administrative suspension proceedings, but rather is intended to spark some ideas which may lead to a challenge of the proceedings in your jurisdiction.

## II. Guiding Principle: constitutional guarantees apply

No state shall make or enforce any law which shall abridge the privilege or immunities of citizens of the United States; nor shall any State deprive any person of life, liberty, or property without due process of law; nor deny to any person within its jurisdiction the equal protection of the laws.
— FOURTEENTH AMENDMENT OF THE UNITED STATES CONSTITUTION

There can be no doubt that the suspension of a driver's license constitutes the deprivation of a constitutionally protected property interest, thus invoking the requirements of due process. In *Bell v. Burson*, 402 U.S. 535, 539, 91 S. Ct. 1586, 29 L. Ed. 2d 90 (1971), a motorist challenged Georgia's requirement that uninsured motorists involved in an accident pay a security deposit in the amount of the damages claimed or have their driver's licenses suspended. The motorist, who happened to be a minister, argued that his due process rights were violated under the statute because he had no opportunity for a hearing on the issue of liability prior to the suspension of his license.

The United States Supreme Court held that once driver's licenses are issued "their continued possession may become essential in the pursuit of a livelihood." Because of their value, the Court held they "are not to be taken away without that procedural due process required by the Fourteenth Amendment." *Bell*, 29 L. Ed. 2d at 94.

In determining what process was due, the Court noted that different situations require different levels of due process. Due process, it held, does not automatically require a full adjudicatory hearing. The Court addressed the due process requirements under the statutory scheme being challenged, but left the particulars of meeting the limited hearing requirements to the individual states. This, then, becomes the focus of Fourteenth Amendment challenges to administrative suspension proceedings.

A few years later, the United States Supreme Court was faced with the issue of whether a statute that required suspension of a driver's license for refusal to submit to a breath test violated the due process clause of the Fourteenth Amendment. *Mackey v. Montrym*, 443 U.S. 1, 99 S. Ct. 2612, 61 L. Ed. 2d 321 (1979). Under the law, the driver could have received an immediate hearing after surrendering his license, though none was requested. The Supreme Court noted that because a driver's license was a "protectable property interest," the only issue left was to decide how much process was due.

In so doing, the Court looked back to the test established in *Mathews v. Eldridge*, 424 U.S. 319, 96 S. Ct. 893, 47 L. Ed. 2d 18 (1976). Those factors are: (1) the private interest that will be affected by the official action; (2) the risk of an erroneous deprivation of such interest through the procedures used; and (3) the Government's interest, including the function involved and the fiscal and administrative burdens, that the additional or substitute procedural requirement would entail." *Mathews*, 47 L. Ed. 2d at 33.

The court examined these factors through a balancing test and found that although the motorist's interest in his driver's license was substantial, the State's interest in highway safety justified the summary suspension of privileges, pending the result of a post-supension hearing. It emphasized that under this statutory scheme, motorists had a right to a "same day" hearing on the matter. After balancing the factors, the Court upheld the constitutionality of the implied consent statute.

In these types of cases, the private interest is the license to operate the vehicle. "[T]hat interest is a substantial one, for the Commonwealth will not be able to make a driver whole for any personal inconvenience and any economic hardship suffered by reason of any delay in redressing an erroneous suspension through post-suspension review procedures." *Mackey*, 433 U.S. at 11. The Court, however, found that the risk is not so great so as to automatically render an automatic suspension proceeding, which is followed by a fair hearing, unconstitutional.

The factor involving the risk or erroneous deprivation is analyzed depending on whether a full hearing, after automatic suspension, is available. If so, the Court has found that the risk of error inherent in the suspension procedure is not so substantial to require an evidentiary hearing. "[E]ven though our legal tradition regards the adversary process as the best means of ascertaining truth and minimizing the risk of error, the 'ordinary principle' established by our prior decisions is that 'something less than an evidentiary hearing is sufficient prior to adverse administrative action.'" *Mackey*, 443 U.S. at 13.

Finally, the Government's interest is viewed in terms of highway safety. The Court found that the summary suspension procedure in Massachusetts served substantial public interests because it acted as a deterrent to drunk driving, it provided an inducement to take the breath analysis test, and it summarily removed from the road licensees arrested for drunk driving who refused to submit to the test. "A state has the right to offer incentives for taking the breath-analysis test and, in exercising its police powers, is not required by the Due Process Clause to adopt an all or nothing approach to the acute safety hazard posed by drunk drivers." *Mackey*, 99 S. Ct. at 2620–21.

Following these Supreme Court decisions, most state challenges to the administrative hearings regarding suspension of driving privileges have focused on whether the challenged procedure was similar enough to the procedures previously examined by the Supreme Court to warrant upholding the statutory scheme. The key elements that have emerged necessary for administrative proceedings to be upheld are: (1) an arrest; (2) a sworn report of the officer who requested the chemical test; (3) a hearing if requested by the motorist; and (4) a temporary license until the hearing is provided.

To effectively challenge an implied consent hearing procedure, counsel should examine the state statutory procedures to determine whether motorists are provided these elements, as well as provided a meaningful, fair suspension hearing.

## III. Applications

### A. DELAYED HEARING AS DENIAL OF DUE PROCESS

Most of the suspension statutes contain time limitations during which the suspension hearing, if requested, is to be held. Although the language of these statutes often sounds mandatory — and jurisdictional — courts often find that they are directory and that the State's failure to hold the hearing in a timely manner does not violate the motorist's rights.

For example, in *Texas Dept. of Public Safety v. Vela*, 980 S.W.2d 672 (Tex. App. 1998), the court held that although the legislature probably intended for the suspension hearing to be held within 40 days, this time requirement was directory rather than mandatory. The court noted that every effort should be made to hold the hearing within the statutory 40 days, but that the time could be extended, for good cause shown.

When a "good cause" loophole exists for the State, however, defense counsel should be diligent in making sure that the State meets this standard of excuse. For example, under a statutory scheme where a hearing must be held within a specified number of days unless "good cause" is shown for a continuance, the licensee may be entitled to cross-examine the person claiming that "good cause" existed.

This was the situation in *Miller v. Tanaka*, 80 Hawaii 358, 910 P.2d 129 (Hawaii App. 1995), *cert. denied*, 80 Hawaii 357, 910 P.2d 128 (1996). The hearing was supposed to be held within 25 days of the mailing of the suspension notice. It was scheduled for day 23 but the hearing officer continued the hearing until day 43. In so doing, he marked on a pre-printed continuance form that the "good cause" was the unavailability of the hearing officer because of illnesss/family emergency. The licensee sought to subpoena the person granting the continuance in order to challenge whether other hearing officers were available, what the other schedules were like for the rest of the day and the rest of the week, etc. The appellate court found that the refusal to issue this subpoena — in order to determine whether the hearing was held in a timely manner — deprived the licensee of his due process rights.

Another example of holding the State to its time deadlines is *Higgins v. Motor Vehicles Division,* 139 Or. App. 314, 911 P.2d 950 (1996). In *Higgins,* the hearing was continued beyond the specified time because the officer certified that he had an official duty conflict. This type of conflict was statutorily defined as arising when, for example, an officer had "priority training." The officer in this case had only certified that he was in training — not in "priority training" and so, the court held, there was not an adequate basis for delaying the hearing past the statutory 30 days.

Another key to increasing the chances of success in arguments based on delay of proceedings is to be able to demonstrate how the licensee was harmed by the delay in the hearing. Creativity (and the facts) are the only limits on this argument. Here are some ways in which drivers are sometimes prejudiced by the seizure of that little plastic rectangle, even if they have temporary driving privileges:

- Unable to rent a car
- Unable to satisfy photo ID requirements needed to board an airplane
- Unable to enter any federal enclave
- Unable to cash a check
- Unable to satisfy document requirements for some employment
- Unable to obtain auto insurance
- Unable to apply for bank loan

B. LIMITATION OF ISSUES AT HEARING

Most state administrative suspension statutes limit the issues which may be raised or addressed at the administrative hearing. These limitations may provide the basis for a challenge based on due process. In *Javed v. Department of Public Safety,* 921 P.2d 620

(Alaska 1996), the motorist challenged the ruling of the hearing officer that prohibited him from presenting evidence that he had not been driving the vehicle. The hearing officer barred this evidence because it did not fall within one of the issues set forth in the statute: whether the officer had reasonable grounds to believe that the accused was operating the vehicle.

The Alaska court held that the limiting language in the statute denied the driver of a meaningful hearing because the issue of whether he was driving is of central importance. In arriving at this decision, the court noted that in determining whether there has been a meaningful hearing, the court must be guided by considerations of fundamental fairness. *Id.* at 266. "It is hard to imagine an issue of more 'central importance' to a driver's license revocation hearing than whether the person accused of DWI was driving a vehicle in the first place." *Id.* at 623. "Due process requires that an arrestee who fails a breath test must be afforded the opportunity at an administrative revocation hearing to present evidence that he was not driving in order to make that hearing meaningful and fundamentaly fair." *Id.* at 624. The court ultimately held that because of the limiting language, the statute was unconstitutional.

### C. RIGHT OF CROSS-EXAMINATION

Many states have administrative proceedings at which the arresting officer is not required to appear and the hearing officer simply relies on his written — sworn or unsworn — report. This has been an area in which due process challenges have been frequent and have had a measure of success — particularly when cross-examination has been limited. The courts still tend to find that hearsay statements — particularly in sworn statements — are sufficent and not violative of due process, so long as the accused has the right to subpoena the law enforcement officers involved.

For example, in *Department of Revenue and Taxation v. Hull,* 751 P.2d 351 (Wyo. 1988), the court found that although the arresting officer's implied consent form may be admitted as an exception to the hearsay rule and can be used as dispositive evidence, due process is satisfied if the hearing officer affords the driver an opportunity to secure the attendence of the police officer.

Similarly, in *Carson v. Division of Vehicles, Kansas Department of Revenue,* 237 Kan. 166, 699 P.2d 447 (1985), the Kansas Supreme Court held that the challenged license suspensions were void as violations of due process because the affidavits relied upon contained only the officer's conclusions, but did not contain facts showing the arresting officer had reasonable grounds under the Fourth Amendment to believe that prior to arrest, the drivers were operating the vehicles under the influence of alcohol. The court held that although the State could proceed on the sworn affidavits, it had to include sufficient facts for the hearing officer to make a determination of whether the facts supported a finding of reasonable grounds.

Further, the court emphasized that the accused had a right to request that subpoenas be issued for the officers. "We recognize that to require the officer's presence at every hearing would not only be an unreasonable expense to the taxpayers, but, in many cases, would be totally unnecessary and an unreasonable burden upon both law enforcement officials and the KDR. . . . Of course, if the licensee requests the presence of the officer, or any other relevant witness, subpoenas are required to be issued for them." *Id.* at 454–55.

Some courts have found, however, that reliance on even sworn reports does not comport with due process. For example in *Thomas v. Fiedler,* 700 F. Supp. 1527 (E.D. Wis. 1988), the hearing officer relied on the sworn report of the arresting officer. The hearing officer would review the reports for the presence of evidence on each of six statutory factors that could be raised and then would accept the police report "as the true recitation of events and continue the suspension." *Fiedler,* 700 F. Supp. at 1538. This, along with other procedural irregularities, led to a finding of a denial of due process.

Despite the seemingly obvious denial of due process attendant with proceeding on written reports, some jurisdictions have found this to be acceptable. See, e.g., *Brouillette v. Department of Public Safety,* 589 So. 2d 529 (La. App. 1991) (hearsay evidence is acceptable so long as it possesses probative value commonly accepted by reasonably prudent men in the conduct of their affairs); *Gray v. Adduci,* 73 N.Y.2d 741, 532 N.E.2d 1268 (N.Y. 1988) (hearsay evidence may be basis of an administrative license revocation); *Department of Revenue and Taxation v. Hull,* 751 P.2d 351 (Wyo.

1988) (police implied consent form is an exception to the hearsay rule because it is a public record and thus may be introduced in evidence at administrative hearing).

Even in jurisdictions in which it is acceptable to proceed on written documents, however, care should be taken to be certain that the reports strictly comply with any and all statutory or regulatory requirements. Any failure to comply should be vigorously challenged. This was done with great success in *Shea v. Department of Motor Vehicles,* 62 Cal. App. 4th 1057, 72 Cal. Rptr. 2d 896 (Cal. App. 4 Dist. 1998). There, forensic alcohol reports were allowed into evidence, as official records of the DMV. These reports fell within a hearsay exception for reports prepared by public employees within the scope of their employment duties. The forensic reports in question were signed by forensic alcohol analyst trainees. The court found that trainees, who were required to be supervised, could not conduct the tests in scope of their employment. In addition, the court found it to be a material misrepresentation, that these trainees signed the reports as analysts, when in fact they were trainees. This was an additional reason to not allow the reports to be admitted. "[A]s Lord Light, the fictional English judge created by A.P. Herbert put it in *Rex v. Haddock,* 'it is like the thirteenth stroke of a crazy clock, which not only is itself discredited but casts a shade of doubt over all previous assertions.' " *Id.* at 898, quoting Herbert, *Uncommon Law* (Eyre Methuen Ltd. 1978, p.28).

In addition to the issue of reliance on reports, the accused should also be allowed to cross-examine the officer on any relevant issue. Failure to allow vigorous cross-examination results in a denial of due process. For example, in *Coracci v. Commissioner of Motor Vehicles,* 42 Conn. Super. 599, 634 A.2d 924 (Conn. Super. 1993), the court found that the hearing officer's failure to allow the motorist's attorney to question an officer about the repair and certification records of the Intoximeter 3000 used to test his client denied the defendent due process. The court noted that the condition of the testing device was highly relevant to the issues at hand and that to deny counsel the chance to question the reliability of the tests performed on him was a denial of due process.

Likewise, in *Barcott v. State Department of Public Safety,* 741 P.2d 226 (Alaska 1987), the motorist was prohibited, at the suspension hearing, from offering any evidence concerning the margin of error inherent in the breath testing procedure. The court held that the accused in a license revocation proceeding has the constitutionally guaranteed right to challenge the accuracy of the breath test independently. "We have thus concluded that due process will not allow the results of a chemical test . . . to be conclusively presumed accurate." *Id.* at 230.

### D. RIGHT TO ISSUE SUBPOENAS/DISCOVERY

As noted above, courts have "expanded" what type of evidence is allowed in the administrative hearing by consoling the accused with assurances that he can subpoena the officer if he wished to contest the contents of the report. It is critical, then, for counsel to fully exercise this right — as it is one of the few positions of power available during the administrative process. Being able to cross-examine the officer at the administrative hearing — which most generally occurs before the officer has "consulted" with the prosecuting attorney — can produce a wealth of information and should not be a missed opportunity.

The courts have generally found that the right to cross-examine witnesses — and thus subpoena them — exists even in the administrative forum. For example, in *Thomas v. Fielder*, 700 F. Supp. 1527 (E.D. Wis. 1988), the court discussed a number of challenges to the administrative hearings under an implied consent statute. One of the factors noted by the court was that the agency's regulation prohibited the arresting officer from being subpoenaed. The court found that not allowing such a subpoena to issue — along with other problems in the statutory scheme — violated due process.

In addition, if a licensee has a regulatory or statutory right to request that subponeas be issued, and attempts to do so, but none is issued, this violates his due process rights. In *Nye v. Department of Revenue*, 902 P.2d 959 (Colo. App. 1995), the court held that because the department had ignored the motorist's request for subpoenas, his due process rights had been violated. The court noted that cross-examination is a fundamental right, even in administrative proceedings, and found that regardless of the driver's likelihood of success at the hearing, he was entitled to have the witnesses subpoenaed to the hearing. *Id.* at 961–62.

Similarly, in *Miller v. Tanaka*, 80 Hawaii 358, 910 P.2d 129

(Hawaii App. 1995), *cert. denied,* 80 Hawaii 357, 910 P.2d 128 (Hawaii 1996), the court held that the failure of the department to issue the subpoenas requested by the licensee was an abuse of discretion, denying the licensee of his due process rights. But, it is important to exercise this right — or it is lost. For example, in *People v. Johnson,* 186 Ill. App. 3d 951, 542 N.E.2d 1226 (1989), the court held that because the accused had failed to exercise his right to subpoena the officers, the case could proceed on only the sworn reports of the officers, when the officers did not voluntarily appear at the hearing.

Discovery of "things" — reports, videotapes, etc. — are also an important function of the administrative hearing, that should be covered by due process concepts. For example, the Alaska Supreme Court found that the State had the duty to preserve a videotape of the accused performing field sobriety tests so that the licensee could contest, at the revocation hearing, whether the officer had reasonable grounds to believe he was under the influence of alcohol. *Thorne v. Department of Public Safety,* 774 P.2d 1326, 1329 (Alaska 1989). The court noted that the accused at a revocation hearing "must be granted the opportunity to fully contest issues of central importance of the revocation decision." *Id.* at 1331.

Even if other discovery methods are blocked in the administrative hearing proceedings, counsel may try to obtain useful information through the State's Open Records Act or the Freedom of Information Act (FOIA). . . .

E. RIGHT TO COUNSEL

Generally, there is no right to counsel, appointed or retained, in a civil proceeding. Because revocation proceedings are based on the same set of facts as criminal proceedings, however, the two proceedings are closely linked; therefore, arguably, the criminal right to appointed counsel should attach to the civil administrative proceedings. Because the United States Supreme Court has held that the criminal right to counsel attaches only in criminal proceedings that can lead to actual imprisonment, any claim to counsel must be framed in terms of the argument that the proceeding is sufficiently analogous to, and intertwined with, the criminal DUI charge, that the appointment of counsel is warranted.

In *Friedman v. Commissioner of Public Safety,* 473 N.W.2d 828 (Minn. 1991), the court recognized a motorist's limited state constitutional right to counsel before chemical testing. The driver's license was revoked for refusal to submit to testing, and on appeal she challenged the revocation on the theory that she was denied her right to counsel prior to the testing. The court interpreted the Minnesota constitution as providing a limited right to counsel that attaches once an officer asks a motorist to submit to testing.

Most courts have rejected right to counsel arguments and have applied the rule that there is no right to counsel, appointed or otherwise, in civil proceedings. For example, in *People v. Golden,* 117 Ill. App. 3d 150, 453 N.E.2d 15 (Ill. App. 1983), the motorist argued that the administrative suspension hearing was a critical stage in the drinking/driving proceedings because the issues and evidence in both the civil and criminal proceedings were sufficiently similar to make the implied consent hearing a critical stage. The motorist further complained that an unrepresented motorist could make incriminating statements at the administrative hearing that might later be introduced at the criminal proceeding.

All of these arguments were rejected by the court. It held that the implied consent hearing is independent from the criminal prosecution and noted the differences in the two proceedings, including the issues addressed and the burdens of proof. It also rejected the claim that the motorist could be prejudiced in the criminal proceedings by findings in the civil proceedings. The court also dismissed the argument that counsel should be appointed because incriminating statements might be made, finding that acceptance of this argument would result in the necessity of appointing counsel in any matter concerning an indigent person. Although these challenges have not met with great success, the argument still exists. Noted DUI defense experts and authors Flem Whited and Donald Nichols include the following points to consider, raise, and argue, in their treatise, *Drinking/Driving Litigation Criminal and Civil* (2d ed. § 11.6):

(1)  Can a public defender protect a defendant's rights if the implied consent proceedings are held prior to the final adjudication of the criminal case?

(2)  In states that have recognized the right to counsel prior

to the election of a test, does a person have the right to a public defender before making the election?

(3) Does the "civil" label attached to the implied consent proceedings realistically reflect the quasi-criminal nature of the implied consent statute?

(4) Does effective assistance of counsel require a public defender to use the implied consent procedure to prepare the drinking/driving case?

(5) Can a public defender advise a defendant with regard to the defendant's rights in the implied consent hearing? Furthermore, does the public defender have a duty to explain the complex interrelationship between the implied consent law and the drinking/driving law?

## F. FAIRNESS OF HEARING OFFICER

A possible challenge to the administrative implied consent proceedings may be based on the separations of functions argument. Routinely, hearing officers work for the same agency which is seeking to suspend the accused's driver's license. Clearly established law requires that an impartial decisionmaker is essential to an administrative adjudication that comports with due process, even if *de novo* review is available. See, e.g., *Withrow v. Larkin,* 421 U.S. 35, 95 S. Ct. 1456, 43 L. Ed. 2d 712 (1975); *Gibson v. Berryhill,* 411 U.S. 564, 93 S. Ct. 1689, 36 L. Ed. 2d 488 (1973); *Butler v. Department of Public Safety & Corr.,* 609 So. 2d 790 (La. 1992).

The Louisiana Supreme Court rejected such a challenge in *Butler,* but it should be noted that under that statutory scheme, the State Administrative Procedures Act attempted to prevent partiality or bias in adjudicative settings by prohibiting *ex parte* consultations and requiring recusal of subordinate deciding officers or agency members from proceedings in which they could not afford a fair and impartial hearing. In so doing, the Louisiana court noted that the United States Supreme Court has placed the burden on the party challenging the constitutionally of an administrative ajudication for bias to overcome the strong presumption of honesty and integrity in those serving as hearing officers. "That party must present convincing evidence that the combination of functions in the same individuals poses such a risk of actual and substantial bias or prejudgment that the practice must be forbidden if the guarantee of due process is to be preserved." *Id.* at 793.

The Louisiana court identified five possible kinds of "bias" calling the decisionmaker's impartiality into question: (1) a prejudgment or point of view about a question of law or policy; (2) a prejudgment about legislative facts that help answer a question of law or policy; (3) advance knowledge of adjudicative facts that are in issue; (4) a personal bias or personal prejudice — an attitude towards a person, as distinguished from an attitude about an issue; and (5) one who stands to gain or lose by a decison either way or a conflict of interest. *Id.* at 794–95. See also, *Department of Highway Safety v. Stewart,* 625 S. 2d 123 (Fla. App. 5 Dist. 1933) (fact that hearing offices are fellow employees of highway patrol troopers does not result in an inherently unfair or unconstitutional hearing).

Thus, although a combination of functions is not a due process violation, per se, this argument still does exist when there is evidence — perhaps statistical or anecdotal — to overcome the presumption of propriety. Be creative when looking for evidence of bias: has the hearing officer received an award from a local MADD chapter as a champion of victims' rights? Does he attend training sessions put on by law enforcement agencies? Consider using your state's Open Records Act or FOIA to obtain copies of attendance lists of those participating in law enforcement sponsored seminars. . . .

## G. Non-attorney as Hearing Officer

In some jurisdictions, the hearing officer is not required to be a licensed attorney. Does it deny the motorist of his due process rights if the person adjudicating the merits of legal motions and arguments has not been trained in the law?

In *Tremain v. State,* 343 So. 2d 819 (Fla. 1977), the court addressed the issue of whether it violated due process protections to have a non-lawyer judge presiding in a misdemeanor case. The motorist argued that the expertise of the professional attorney is wasted if his forensic challenges are directed toward a judge "who has no more educational background to absorb and apppreciate such arguments than any spectators in the courtroom gallery." The court agreed, in theory, saying: "[I]t is clear that a judge who is ignorant of the law cannot afford due process of law to an individual facing imprisonment upon conviction." *Id.* at 823. It went on, however, to find that if the hearing officer successfully completed the state's system for training non-lawyer judges, that would be sufficient to satisfy due process.

### IV.  Conclusion

There can be no doubt of the devastating impact that a suspension of driving privileges can have on a client's family, financial situation, community involvement, and recreation. As Justice Stewart said in his dissent in *Mackey,* "Even a day's loss of a driver's license can inflict grave injury upon a person who depends upon an automobile for continued employment in his job." 443 U.S. at 30. Although constitutional challenges to the administrative suspension proceedings are an uphill battle, because of the dire consequences of suspension hearings, they are worth considering, evaluating, and developing.

---

## §3.3   The Refusal Suspension

### §3.3.5   Attempts to "Cure" a Refusal

*Page 158.  Add new section after end of subsection 3.3.5:*

### §3.4   The FAA and Pilot License Suspensions

Counsel may well encounter the client who is a pilot and for whom the loss of his pilot's license presents greater concern than the loss of his driver's license and/or criminal conviction. For a commercial pilot, it may well represent the end of a rewarding career — at least, if improperly handled by an attorney not familiar with Federal Aviation Administration regulations and procedures. It may also represent potential grounds for a legal malpractice action.

The following material will give the DUI practitioner sufficient information to at least be aware of some of the pitfalls in advising or representing a pilot who has been arrested for drunk driving. The author is grateful to J. Gary Trichter (a Houston DUI attorney with a pilot's license and the owner of three airplanes) and Christian Samuelson for their contribution.*

---

Captain Lucky Lindy, a 15-year major-airline pilot with 15,000 flight hours and who is also a United States Air Force Reserve Flight Officer of 19 years, tells you that 16 days ago he was not so lucky as he was arrested for drunk driving by a member of the local constabulary. He apologizes for not coming in sooner, but he had been on a weeklong round-trip flight out of the country and had to immediately report for military reserve duty upon his return. Unlucky Lindy then informs you that he refused the Intoxiliar breath test and he is very concerned that this incident might cause him to be forced into early retirement. The client's high level of stress is clearly manifested in his voice and by the fact that he continually asks for assurances that he is not going to lose his lifetime investment in his aviation career. Reassuring him that he will be all right and that he is in the best of hands, you schedule an afternoon appointment for him.

Not being a pilot or a person with any real aviation experience, you call a local flight school to ask what is the Federal Aviation Adminstration (FAA) reporting requirement for DWI/DUI. A young certified flight instructor (CFI) first tells you that there are three types of pilot medical certificates, i.e., a first class that is good for six months, a second class that is good for 12 months, and a third class that is good for 24 months. He further explains that all pilots must have a current medical certificate in order to be legal to fly. The CFI then said the only requirement that he knew about concerning a DWI/DUI conviction was that it be admitted in the space provided for it on the medical certificate application form. Feeling somewhat better informed, you thank the youngster, say good-bye and wait for your new client to arrive.

At your office interview later that day, Lindy tells you that his FAA First Class Medical Certificate will expire in two weeks and then requests your advice as to whether or not he needs to report his arrest to the feds. Not knowing about the Federal Aviation Regulations (FARS), you tell him not to worry, that you will do

---

*Reprinted with permission.

some research into the matter, and have an answer for him soon.

During the interview, you properly and thoroughly explain that his case is very defendable, that a DWI/DUI first offense, if there is a conviction, could theoretically result in a sentence of jail, a fine, both jail and a fine, and a driver's license suspension of up to one year. You further inform him that as a consequence of his breath-test refusal and because he missed the 15-day period after his arrest to request an administrative hearing, he will lose his driver's license for 90 days. The good news, however, is that he is eligible for an occupational license and that it is almost a sure thing the court will grant him one during the three month suspension period.

Unlucky Lindy again revisits the questions with you as to "how will all this affect my flying?" and "do I have to report this to the FAA at this time or later?" Exactly how you answer this question will make a big difference to your legal malpractice carrier, if you have one, and to your retirement account if you do not have coverage. More importantly, it will make all the professional and emotional difference in the world to your pilot client.

Remembering the CFI's quick tutorial, you inform the client that it is your opinion the medical certificate form only requires the reporting of "convictions" so there is no need to make reference of the arrest on the form when he applies for a new medical certificate. Fortunately, for you, that information is correct. You then say that it is your opinion that the FAA need not be notified at all unless there is a conviction. Oops! This advice just caused a "disturbance in the Force," as it is incorrect. Section 61.15 of the FARS is what caused the disturbance. It provides:

*Offenses involving alcohol or drugs* . . .

(c) For the purposes of . . . this section, a motor vehicle action means:

(1) A conviction after November 29, 1990, for the violation of any Federal or State statute relating to the operation of a motor vehicle while intoxicated by alcohol or a drug; while impaired by alcohol or a drug, or while under the influence of alcohol or a drug;

(2) The cancellation, suspension or revocation of a license

to operate a motor vehicle after November 29, 1990, for a *cause related* to the operation of a motor vehicle while intoxicated by alcohol or a drug, or while under the influence of alcohol or a drug, [emphasis added]; . . .

(d) Except for a motor vehicle action that results from the same incident or arises out of the same factual circumstances, a motor vehicle action occurring within three years of a previous motor vehicle action is grounds for: . . .
(2) Suspension or revocation of any certificate, rating, or authorization issued under this part. . . .

(e) Each person holding a certificate issued under this part shall provide a written report of each motor vehicle action to the FAA, Civil Action Security Division (AMC-700), P.O. Box 25810, Oklahoma City, OK 73125, not later than 60 days after the motor vehicle action. The report must include:
(1) The person's name, address, date of birth, and airman certificate number;
(2) The type violation that resulted in the conviction or the administrative action;
(3) The date of the conviction or administrative action;
(4) The State that holds the record of the conviction or administrative action; and
(5) A statement of whether the motor vehicle action resulted from the same incident or arose out of the same factual circumstances related to a previously reported motor vehicle action . . .

(f) Failure to comply with paragraph (e) of this section is grounds for . . .
(2) Suspension or revocation of any certificate, rating, or authorization issued under this part.

Your incorrect advice could cause client Lindy to have his pilot's license suspended or revoked if he does not notify the FAA Civil Aviation Security Division not later than 60 days after his driver's license goes into suspension for refusing to submit to the Intoxiliar test. Of course, should Lindy lose his pilot's license then he most likely would lose his job, too, and you will inevitably get sued! Ouch!

Let's change the facts a bit so that Unlucky Lindy comes to

you and says he simply wants to plead guilty, get probation, and get this unfortunate episode behind him. He then asks, "Will it be sufficient to report my plea and conviction by affirmatively noting them on my medical certificate application?" If you are inclined to think that it is logical to assume the answer is "yes" because your client is actually notifying the FAA of his conviction by admitting it on the form, then you should be happy to know it is indeed a logical conclusion. Regrettably, however, like the rest of the government, the FAA does not always think, act, or promulgate its rules logically, and again you should feel a "disturbance in the Force."

If you don't like that answer or you do not believe in the "Force," then consider the bureaucratic nightmare that befell a major-airline captain in 1991. In May the pilot was arrested for drunk driving. Days after his arrest, feeling very concerned about his career and about following the rules, he actually called the local FAA office (Flight Standards District Office a/k/a "FSDO") to ask about the affect the DUI/DWI would have on his pilot's license. The FSDO, being helpful, only reminded him that it would be necessary to report the conviction, if one happened, on his medical application form when he reapplied for it the next month in June.

Not wishing to contest the DUI/DWI, the captain pled guilty on June 10. Within two weeks, during the completion of his medical application form, the captain in answer to question "21v" checked "yes" and self-disclosed the conviction. Notwithstanding the fact that he did not make further reference to the conviction on the form, he did explain and further disclose the events giving rise to the conviction to the FAA Medical Examiner Physician. The doctor, ostensibly believing the captain fit for flying, issued him a new medical certificate.

On the first of October, the FAA's Aeromedical Branch, following routine procedures, requested the captain to furnish further details of the conviction. The information was promptly furnished to the satisfaction of the branch.

Then comes the "disturbance in the Force." The FAA popped the captain for a 20-day suspension for violating FAR 61.15 because he did not specifically notify the Civil Aviation Security Division in Oklahoma City within the 60 days, as called for by the rule. "Wow!" you say? Well, so said the captain too! "Unreasonable!" you say? Well, you must be clairvoyant because that is exactly what the dumbfounded captain also said.

Does the word "appeal" come to mind? It did to the captain and he appealed to the National Transportation Safety Board (NTSB) saying in effect that because he had no intent to deceive and that he had in fact reported his conviction to the FAA, although not to the security division because he was unaware of the rule, it was unreasonable to find a violation and suspend him. "Wow!" said the judge agreeing with the pilot. "Unreasonable!" said the judge again agreeing with the pilot. Indeed, after hearing the evidence the judge not only found that there was "substantial compliance" with the rule, but also, he dismissed the case against the pilot.

Does the word "appeal" come to mind again? It did to the FAA and it appealed to the full five-member NTSB Board. "Wow!" said the Board. "Reversed" said the Board, and they reinstated the record of the conviction albeit without the suspension. The Board went on to say that, *"[a]s a general rule, airmen are expected and obliged to know the regulations to which they are subject, and ignorance of them is no defense. The reporting requirement regulation was in effect at the time of the [captain's conviction] and its language is absolutely clear"* [emphasis added]. "Ouch!" said the captain. His lawyer probably said, "HOLY S–T!!!!!!!!!!"

The above examples ought to make you very careful in representing pilots in drunk driving prosecutions and/or administrative driver's license proceedings that are collateral to the drunk driving case. Clearly, the effect of either a failure to report or even a properly filed report are quite consequential for the pilot. Clearly, too, if that effect was brought about by ignorance and improper advice of counsel then, it too, has serious consequences for the lawyer.

Unquestionably, FAR 61.15 is a landmine just waiting to get stepped on by the innocent pilot/client and the unwary lawyer. One would think if the self-disclosure requirement were that important to the FAA that it would have created a form for reporting the required information just as it did on the medical certificate application. That, however, is not the case because there is no preprinted form.

To summarize, the pilot/client who is convicted of DUI/DWI must report that conviction on his medical application. He must also notify the FAA Civil Security Division in Oklahoma City within 60 days of the conviction. Contacting the local FAA FSDO is not compliance under the rule. The pilot/client must also report any action taken on his driver's license that emanated from the drunk driving arrest, i.e., a suspension for either failing the breath/blood test or for refusing a breath/blood test. This report, too, is made to the FAA Oklahoma Office Civil Security Division and must be made within 60 days of the suspension. In cases where the pilot/client suffers both a DUI/DWI conviction as well as an administrative license suspension that arose out of the same factual circumstances, he must timely report both of them to the Security Division or face a non-reporting violation. Note, however, that only one of the two reports can be used for suspension/revocation purposes under FAR 61.15 (d), i.e., the FAA needs two separate incidents within a three-year period to deny an application or suspend/revoke a pilot license.

Playing lawyers for the moment, arguably the reporting requirement for both a conviction and/or a suspension for refusing and/or failing a breath/blood test is in our opinion stayed for as long as the conviction and/or suspension are on appeal. There is no law on this question as of yet, but the 60-day clock on appeals we have handled has been treated by the FAA as starting when the appellate process was over and there were actual final court orders in effect.

Playing lawyers again, from a strategy viewpoint, in many jurisdictions it may be advantageous in defendable DUI/DWI prosecutions where the pilot/client plans on contesting the charge to always appeal the loss of an administrative driver's license revocation/suspension hearing. This is true because in many jursidictions, the license suspension is rescinded as a matter of law where the criminal case ends with a verdict of "not guilty." Clearly, this strategy will prevent you and your client from having to deal with the FAA on the issue of record correction and/or expungement. Said another way, it is a lot easier not to ring the bell in the first instance than it would be to un-ring it after the fact.

Let's stroll through the minefield with two more examples before we put this topic to rest. Example 1: How about where the pilot/client is arrested for drunk driving, he refuses the Intoxiliar test, DUI/DWI charges are filed but subsequently dismissed for insufficient evidence; however, he still suffers a driver's license suspension for the breath test refusal. Looking at FAR 61.15(c)(2), the quesion becomes: does the not so clear language: "... for a cause related to the operation of a motor vehicle *while intoxicated*..." excuse such a pilot from the self-reporting requirement because there was not sufficient evidence of "while intoxicated" to warrant a continued drunk driving prosecution [emphasis added]?

Applying the NTSB logic about "language [that] is absolutely clear" from our first example, a reasonable pilot and/or reader should clearly interpret the " while intoxicated" language of FAR 61.15(c)(2) to mean what it says, i.e., that there must be sufficient evidence that the driver *was intoxicated* to require him to notify the Civil Aviation Security Division. Requiring that a statute, rule, regulation, or law be interpreted in light of the clear meaning of its words makes good sense to us. Indeed, that has been a judicial and legislative rule of construction for quite some time now. Moreover, one would also think that a reasonable pilot and/or reader could rely on the doctrine of *"stare decisis."* Remember, this is the doctrine that requires consistency so that "we the people" can rely on precedent in order for us to be "expected and obliged to know the regulations to which[we] are subject. ...."

Regrettably, there is no guarantee in life that either the FAA or the NTSB will act logically, reasonably, sensibly, on the clear meaning of a FAR, or on precedent. Such was the hard 120-day pilot's license suspension lesson learned by an Ohio commercial pilot who had been stopped for erratic driving and subsequently refused to submit to a breath test. In that case the pilot was neither arrested nor charged with drunk driving but did suffer a one-year driver's license suspension.

This case turned on the FAA's and NTSB's interpretation of FAR 61.15(d)'s language "motor vehicle action." On the rationale side of the controversy was the pilot who argued that a breath test refusal is not proof of alcohol or drug involvement. Indeed, the definition of "motor vehicle action" requires that the suspension be "for a cause related to the operation of a motor vehicle *while* intoxicated by alcohol or a drug, *while* impaired by alcohol or a drug, or *while* under the influence of alcohol or a drug [emphasis added]." In this regard, it is of import to note that the suspension was not for being intoxicated, but, rather, only for refusing the requested test. Of course on the flip side of the controversy was the FAA, which claimed in a conclusory and wholesale fashion that a breath test refusal fit within the broad meaning of "motor vehicle action" under section 61.15. In a decision that runs afoul with reason and plain language, the NTSB simply deferred to the FAA and rubber-stamped its definition. So much for fairness, uniformity, and *"stare decisis."*

Example 2: Our final example involves the scenario where the pilot/client, although originally charged with DUI/DWI, is allowed to plead to a lesser or new nonintoxication/nonimpairment/noninfluence charge, such as reckless driving, and the original charge is dismissed, or where the DUI/DWI prosecution resolves itself with a pre-trial diversion, deferred adjudication, or probation before judgment, i.e., there is no final conviction. The question here is "whether or not FAR 61.15 requires self-reporting of cases that are resolved without alcohol, drugs, intoxication, impairment, influence or that do not involve a final conviction." The short answer, at least for now, is "no!"

So what does all this mean to the lawyer who represents the client/pilot who is accused of DUI/DWI? It means you need to be really careful to protect your pilot and yourself from collateral dangers that abound to the client because he is subject to a different and additional set of rules than the non-client/pilot due to his winged status. It means that not only do you need to go out and get a copy of the current FARS, but, also, that you need to read and understand them. Review of NTSB decisions is also a must! Don't get trapped! Read and don't hesistate to ask others more knowledgeable for help or advice. A great place to start is the Aircraft Owners and Pilots Association (AOPA). It has a pilot assistance hotline for members at 1-800-USA-AOPA (1-800-872-2572) and a Web site at www.aopa.org.

In closing, those of us who have been lucky enough to represent pilots know that they are some of the greatest clients and nicest friends around. Remember, protecting a pilot's license is protecting your own law license. Avoid the FAA pitfalls. Don't crash and burn.

# II

# EVIDENCE

# 4

## FIELD EVIDENCE

### §4.2  *Appearance and Behavior of Defendant*

#### §4.2.5  Odor of Alcohol on Breath

*Page 185.  Add after third full paragraph:*

Recently, the scientists whose studies became the basis for the "standardized" field sobriety tests conducted another study on the effectiveness of alcohol odor in detecting intoxication. Moskowitz, Burns & Ferguson, Police Officers' Detection of Breath Odors from Alcohol Ingestion, 31(3) Accident Analysis and Prevention 175 (May 1999). These researchers used 20 experienced officers working with 14 subjects who were tested at blood-alcohol concentrations ranging from zero to .13 percent. Over a four-hour period, the officers smelled the subject's breath odor under optimal conditions, with the subjects hidden from view. The conclusions of the study: Odor strength estimates were unrelated to BAC levels; estimates of BAC levels failed to rise above random guesses. Officers were unable to recognize whether the alcohol beverage was beer, wine, bourbon, or vodka. According to the scientists, these results demonstrate that even under optimum clinical conditions, breath odor detection is unreliable.

#### §4.2.6  Slurred Speech

*Page 187.  Add after first full paragraph:*

In fact, even assuming the honesty of the officer that the defendant's speech *was* slurred, there is little evidence that this is symptomatic of intoxication. Impairment of speech is, for example, a common — and sober — reaction to the stress, fear, and nervousness that a police investigation would be expected to engender; fatigue is another well-known cause. However, consider the following excerpt from a recent issue of *Discover* magazine:

> Bartenders, police officers, and hospital workers routinely identify drunks by their slurred speech. Several investigative groups judged the captain of the grounded Exxon Valdez oil tanker to be intoxicated based solely on the sound of his voice in his radio transmissions. But a team led by Harry Holien, a phonetician at the University of Florida, has found that even self-proclaimed experts are pretty bad at estimating people's alcohol levels by the way they talk.
>
> Hollien asked clinicians who treat chemical dependency, along with a group of everyday people, to listen to recordings made by volunteers when they were sober, then mildly intoxicated, legally impaired, and finally, completely smashed. Listeners consistently overestimated the drunkeness of mildly intoxicated subjects. Conversely, they underestimated the alcohol levels of those who were most inebriated. Professionals were little better at perceiving the truth than the ordinary joes. . . .
>
> He thinks his research could encourage police to be more wary of snap judgments: Mild drinkers might come under needless suspicion. . . .

Saunders, News of Science, Medicine and Technology: Straight Talk, 21(10) Discover (Oct. 2000).

## §4.3   Field Sobriety Tests

### §4.3.5   Horizontal Gaze Nystagmus

*Page 216. Add at end of carryover paragraph:*

(For a judicial recognition of 32 non-alcohol related causes of horizontal gaze nystagmus, see *Schultz v. State*, 106 Md. App. 145 (1995).

## §4.4   Preliminary Breath Tests

*Page 231.   Add at end of section:*

Practitioners across the country should be aware of recent developments in California concerning the use of preliminary breath devices — a development that, in the opinion of this author, will rapidly spread nationwide. That state is apparently making plans to use hand-held breath testing devices *as evidential breath test instruments.* In other words, steps have been taken to phase out current PBT devices as well as the evidential machines currently found in police stations and replace them with a single new hand-held unit, which accomplishes the functions of both.

The following is excerpted from a letter forwarded by a member of the California Department of Justice to the *California Association of Toxicologists Newsletter* and printed in its February 1999 edition:

On September 16, 1996, the California Department of Justice sent a letter to manufacturers of breath analyzers outlining a new law enforcement concept that utilizes hand-held breath analyzers as EBTs . . .

. . . The Alcotest 7410 Plus hand-held breath analyzer with "Smart Cal" and PC software, is the result. The Alcotest $7410^{Plus}$ is the smartest, most powerful, and flexible hand-held breath analyzer ever created . . .

The Department will purchase 20 initially with the OTS grant and be placed in one county to demonstrate Title 17 compliance and will then add them to the License of the DOJ, Bureau of Forensic Services. Then another 100 units will replace Bureau Intoxilyzer 5000 complement. Steve Scott, the BFS Blood Alcohol Coordinator, has applied for a $2.5 million OTS grant in the second phase of this continuing grant to place 800 Alcotest Plus units in patrol cars throughout the state.

This California version of the Draeger 7410, the "7410 Plus," varies from the standard model primarily in using a special software — "Smart Cal." With the capacity to give the tests in the field, of course, retrograde extrapolation (see §5.2) will cease to be a significant problem.

There appear, however, to be defects that will render it susceptible to attack. First, it appears that the new device is not currently designed to incorporate a mouth alcohol detector (see §6.2.5). Thus, mouth alcohol (see §6.2) will become an even greater issue. Second, there is also, apparently, only a very primitive RFI detector planned for the device (see §6.3.10). This will be a particular problem in view of the close proximity of the police car's radio transmitter and the officers' walkie-talkies. And, of course, all the usual infirmities of the relatively primitive RBTs apply.

The new units may also provide counsel with a new strategy in trial. Generally, it has been the author's experience that juries are not impressed with small, mobile, hand-held PAS devices — certainly not as impressed as with the large, more complex stationary machines. This is particularly true now that there is little reason for the officer not to bring the Draeger Alcotest in to trial to show the jury — unlike in the existing situation where the jury never sees the evidential machine. Can the hand-held "gizmo" do what a big, complex machine could do? Can this little unit carried around in the officer's pocket — appearing similar to commercially available units selling for only $100–200 — be trusted to analyze blood-alcohol from breath samples? Beyond a reasonable doubt?

### §4.4.2  Defense Use of Favorable PBT Evidence

*Page 239. Add new subsection after end of subsection 4.4.2:*

### §4.4.3  The Alcotest 7410

The Alcotest 7410 is a small battery-powered device, which employs fuel-cell technology to measure blood-alcohol concentration from a breath sample. It is produced in Lubeck, Germany, by Draeger Safety, Inc., manufacturers of the Alcotest 7110 evidentiary breath machine (see §11.5.4); Draeger got into the business by taking over Smith and Wesson's Breathalyzer Division (185 Suttle Street, Suite 105, Durango, CO 81301-7911; 970-385-5555). The device is a recent development that is seeing rapid acceptance nationwide. The California version is planned for statewide distribution within the next three years — and, notably, since it has been certified as an evidentiary machine, it will be admissible in court as evidence of the defendant's actual blood-alcohol concentration.

As was briefly discussed in §4.4, this handheld unit measures ethyl alcohol in the breath by oxidizing it in the fuel cell, thus generating a small electrical current, which is measured over a given time period; the more ethyl alcohol in the breath sample, the greater the oxidation, the more current generated, the higher the reading. A separate printer is available to record the results of tests. Being a fuel-cell device, it is susceptible to numerous problems, including a lack of specificity (see §6.1). Although the unit theoretically will not react with some compounds that register as alcohol on infrared machines (hydrocarbons, organic acids, ketones, common anorganic gases), it will oxidize and thus read as alcohol such compounds as:

1. Aldehydes, such as acetaldehyde, present to varying degrees on the human breath (see §6.1.1);
2. Ethers;
3. Esters; and
4. Alcohols (methanol, propanol, I-propanol).

In fact, many organic substances with oxygen in the functional compound group may react with fuel cells.

Although the 7410 has a mechanism for detecting radio frequency interference (see §6.3.10), it is a fairly primitive system, which appears to be sensitive only to RFI sources within one to two feet of the device. Most notably, however, the device *does not have a "mouth alcohol" detector* — a significant shortcoming in any breath-testing device and one that should provide material for cross-examination (particularly if the officer's 15-minute pretest observation period is suspect, which is likely to be the case if the test is administered in the field).

The device will degenerate inaccuracy due to contamination of surface sites, causing decreased conductivity. For this and other reasons, it has an expected life of three years, and must be calibrated according to manufacturer's specifications at least every six months by a certified technician using a NHTSA-approved wet bath simulator.

In attempting to get states to accept the device for evidentiary purposes as in California, the advantages of the new unit have been set forth in promotional literature:

1. There is no delay in obtaining a test result, thus it "eliminates the 'rising BA' defense";
2. It "keeps the officer on the street";
3. It permits more remote areas to be served;
4. It costs about 1/3 as much as stand alone evidentiary units; and
5. It replaces units such as the Intoxilyzer 5000 that are 10–15 years old.

Note that none of the advantages relate to the accuracy of the device.

Although retrograde extrapolation will become less of an issue with this device, defense counsel should find it an easier machine to attack in trial — if for no other reason than its diminutive size and unimposing appearance (note: unlike the larger evidentiary instruments, there is no reason the device cannot be brought into court and shown to the jury).

The following material from the California Department of Justice presents excerpts from Draeger's manual for technical specifications, evidential operation, maintenance, and troubleshooting. The author is grateful to forensic toxicologist Anne ImObersteg (302 Toyon Avenue, Suite F266, San Jose, CA 95127; 408-272-5696) for providing and discussing these materials.

TECHNICAL SPECIFICATIONS

**Measurement range**
Accurate between 0.000 gm/210L to 0.400 gm/210L

**Ambient conditions for operation**
23° to 104° F ($-5°$ to $+40°$ C)
or $-4°$ ($-20°$ C), if in use for less than 30 minutes and if 600 to 1300 mbar
10 to 98% relative humidity

**Ambient conditions for storage**
$-40°$ to $+149°$ F ($-40°$ tp $+65°$C)
600 to 1300 mbar
10 to 98% relative humidity

## Minimum Sample Requirements

Blowing time       4 to 12 seconds (depending on intensity)
Flow rate           >6 liters/minute
Volume             >1.2 liters

## Measurement accuracy

Reproducible with an ethanol standard:
0 to 0.100%       +/−0.005% gm/210L
  >0.100%       +/− 5% of measured value

## Dimensions

9.0 x 2.8 x 1.3 in (230 x 70 x 34 mm)

## Weight

1.1 lb (0.5 kg)

## Electrical power supply options:

1. Battery pack which holds three (3) rechargeable NiCd batteries

Notes:

NiCd or rechargeable battery packs will provide approximately 300 tests between charges.

Charging time takes 24 hours for full charge.

**LO BAT** warning is displayed when there is approximately 5 minutes of operating time remaining.

### Printer

#### Environmental conditions for operation

32° to 122°F (0° to 50°c)
600 to 1300 mbar
10 to 98% relative humidity

#### Environmental conditions for storage

−40° to 158°F (−40° to 70°C)
600 to 1300 mbar
10 to 98% relative humidity

#### Dimensions

5.6 x 5.3 x 1.9 in (140 x 133 x 48 mm)

#### Weight

1.0 lb (0.5 kg)

**Power supply**

| | |
|---|---|
| Operating voltage: | 9.5V to 17V / 1A |
| Consumption: | 10 W for log printout, 200 mW in standby mode |
| Fuse: | M 1.0 A DIN 41571 91x) |
| Batteries: | LR6 DIN IEC 86 (AA) (2ea) (Usage period at 25°C is approximately 2 years) |

STRUCTURAL DIAGRAM

1. Electronics compartment
2. ON/OFF switch
3. Calibration sticker
4. Mouthpiece holder
5. Yellow ON light/Red warning light
6. Green READY light
7. LCD display

8. Electrical contacts for battery pack connection
9. Battery pack
10. Wrist strap
11. Electrical contacts for NiCd charger
12. Battery pack release button
13. Safety lock tab
14. PC interface

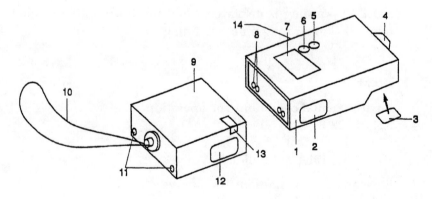

**Printer**

1. Top cover
2. Paper feed slot
3. Paper roll
4. Red button
5. White button

6. Printing mechanism
7. Batteries
8. Power receptacle
9. PC interface

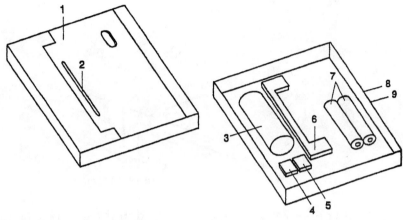

OPERATION

This section explains the operation of the various components of the Draeger *EPAS*. The basic preparation and operation of all components is explained in detail, although the operator will usually not need to do any special preparation to use a properly charged Draeger *EPAS*.

To prepare the Draeger EPAS, simply plug the case into a power source to charge the system batteries. The first time you charge the EPAS, it is recommended to leave it charging for a full 24 hours.

### Alcotest® 7410 *Plus* Operation

This section details the preparation required to use the Alcotest® 7410*Plus*, and the steps for performing a breath test.

Before using the Alcotest® 7410*Plus*, the battery pack must be connected and fully charged.

#### *Connecting the battery pack*

The Alcotest® 7410*Plus* is powered by a rechargeable NiCd battery pack.

**To connect the battery pack:**

1. Pull up the safety lock on the battery pack unit.
2. Position the battery pack unit into the base of the instrument and depress the safety lock.

**To remove the battery pack:**

1. Pull up the safety lock on the battery pack unit.
2. Depress the release button.

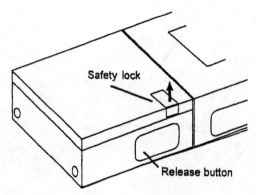

The Alcotest® 7410*Plus* must be charged in the case or charger station whenever **LO BAT** appears at the bottom of the display, or when the NiCd battery is completely exhausted. Below is the procedure to charge the Alcotest® 7410*Plus* using the NiCd charger station of the *EPAS* case.

*To use the NiCd charger station:*

1. Plug in NiCd charger station to power source.
2. Put the rechargeable NiCd battery pack into the charger with the "Power Supply Unit" to the front.
3. When the yellow light in the charger is on, the battery pack unit is being charged.
4. Store the NiCd battery pack in the charger so that it is ready for immediate use.

*Operating the* **EPAS:**

---

*NOTE:* **The Alcotest® 7410***Plus* is always charging while it is in the case. The below instructions are intended for routine maintenance and special situations where the EPAS has been in the field for extended periods of time.

---

1. Leave the battery pack attached to the Alcotest® 7410*Plus*.
2. Place the Alcotest® 7410*Plus* in the special holster inside the *EPAS* case.
3. Plug in the case to a power source, utilizing the correct power cord (110V or 12V).

### *Turning the 7410 on and off*

**ON (for screening tests)**

1. Pick up the Alcotest® 7410*Plus* from the *EPAS* case.
2. Press the ON/OFF button once.

The yellow ON light comes on and a self-test is carried out by the microprocessor. The LCD displays date and time data.

### Evidential Test Procedure

There are two ways to enter data into the Alcotest® 7410*Plus* for an evidential test; with a valid California Driver's License and Operator's Card, or via the Cassiopeia® palm device's virtual keyboard and Jot® system.

### Activating Magnetic Card Data Entry with Cassiopeia®

1. Press the program button on the Cassiopeia® to activate the Data Entry Sequence.
2. Swipe the subject's driver's license through the magnetic card reader as indicated on page 6.
3. Verify that the subject's data has been accepted (The corresponding boxes on the Cassiopeia will turn green).
4. Swipe the Operator's Card through the magnetic card reader.
5. Verify that the operator's data has been accepted (The corresponding boxes on the Cassiopeia will turn green).
6. Select "Upload" from the Cassiopeia's touch screen.

The data is transfered to the Alcotest® 7410*Plus*, which beeps to indicate a successful transfer. The Alcotest® 7410*Plus* is automatically powered on and ready to accept an evidential breath test. The Cassiopeia® will automatically power off after a successful data upload.

### POWER-OFF for the Alcotest® 7410*Plus*

Press the ON/OFF button twice in the Screening mode or Evidential mode.

*Note:* The Alcotest® 7410*Plus* will automatically shut off after four (4) minutes if the unit is in the READY mode and no test has been performed.

### Activating Manual Data Entry with the Cassiopeia®

1. Press the program button on the Cassiopeia® to activate the Data Entry Sequence.
2. On the Cassiopeia® touch screen, tap each box for the subject's data and enter the data with the virtual keyboard or the Jot® system.
3. To enter the operator's data, repeat step 2, tapping the appropriate boxes on the Cassiopeia's touch screen.
4. When all of the data boxes are green, the data is ready to be sent to the Alcotest® 7410*Plus*.
5. Select "Upload" from the Cassiopeia's touch screen.

The data is transferred to the Alcotest® 7410*Plus*, which beeps to indicate a successful transfer. The Alcotest® 7410*Plus* is automatically powered on and ready to accept an evidential breath test. The Cassiopeia® will automatically power off after a successful data upload.

### POWER-OFF for the Alcotest® 7410*Plus*

Press the ON/OFF button twice in the Screening mode or Evidential mode.

*Note:* The Alcotest® 7410*Plus* will automatically shut off after four (4) minutes if the unit is in the READY mode and no test has been performed.

### Performing a Breath Test

**Conditions for test subject** *(follow State requirements)*

*Performing a Screening Test*

Press and release the ON/OFF button once. The 7410 will go through the date sequence,

month               day                year

| nn | 08 | dd | 06 | 'yy | '99 |

followed by the time sequence . . .

hour             minute

| hh | 15 | nn | 45 |

followed by . . .

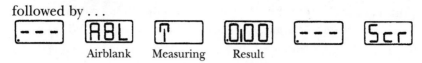

A screening result display sequence with labels: Airblank, Measuring, Result

$\boxed{- - -}$, indicates that the unit is warming up. Once the Alcotest® 7410*Plus* is ready for a Screening Test, the display shows:

$\boxed{Scr}$ and the green "ready" light is on.

A Screening Test can be performed at this point:

Instruct the subject to take a deep breath and blow evenly as long as the horn sounds. If the test was successful the result will automatically be displayed.

> (Note: Display time of the results will vary due to the alcohol concentration measured).

If the subject does not fulfill the volume and flow rate requirements, EO will be displayed, indicating an insufficient breath sample. The test can be repeated when the green "Ready" comes on. This will not change the sequential test number.

All valid test results are stored in the 7410*Plus* memory, including date, time, and sequential test number.

The test results can be printed at this time.

The Alcotest® 7410*Plus* is turned off by pressing the ON/OFF button twice, or it will automatically shut off after four minutes.

**Evidential Testing**

An evidential test can be conducted in the field using the magnetic card reader or the Cassiopeia® for data entry. However, there are situations when an evidential breath test will need to be conducted in a laboratory or station house; for these situations it is also possible to use a PC for data entry. The PC, Card Reader, and Manual Entry protocols are detailed below.

*Performing an Evidential Breath Test with a PC*

Start the Alcotest® 7410*Plus* Upload program on the PC. Enter an access code or swipe the Operator/Supervisor access card through the mag card reader when prompted. The operator will now have the option to "Conduct Evidential Test" or, "Download 7410 Data."

Connect the 7410 to the PC by plugging the RS232 cable into the 7410's PC Interface data port. The 7410 must be turned off.

Swipe the subject's driver's license through the mag card reader, or type in subject data in the appropriate fields.

Next, select violation and press enter.

Then choose City/County and press enter.

If the subject and operator data is correct, select "Upload Data" to send the data to the 7410.

If the Upload was successful, the following messages will be displayed:

> "Connection Successful," followed by "Data Upload Successful" and "Continue Evidential Test By Pressing OK."

The 7410 will start the evidential test sequence by displaying the date:

$$\boxed{nn}, \boxed{08} \boxed{dd}, \boxed{06} \boxed{'yy} \boxed{'99}$$

followed by the time:

$$\boxed{hh} \boxed{15} \boxed{nn}, \boxed{45}$$

followed by: $\boxed{.\,-\,-\,-}$, $\boxed{RBL}$ (Air Blank),

followed by: $\boxed{\top} \quad \boxed{.000}$ (Result).

> Note: If alcohol is detected by the 7410 in the ambient air or the 7410 has not reached .000 from the previous breath test, the 7410 will automatically perform additional Air Blanks until .000 is displayed.

After a successful Air Blank, the 7410 will display $\boxed{.\,-\,-\,-}$, then $\boxed{br1}$ (Breath Test Number 1) followed simultaneously by the horn, green "Ready" light.

Instruct the subject to take a deep beath and blow evenly as long as the horn sounds. If the test was successful the result will automatically be displayed. After 5 seconds the result will be cleared and the following is displayed: $\boxed{- - -}$. The unit will proceed to the second test.

> Note: If the test was not successful, EO will be displayed and the test repeated when the green "Ready" light comes on.

For the second breath test ($\boxed{\mathsf{br2}}$), the above steps will be repeated.

### Evidential Testing with the *EPAS*

There are two ways to conduct an evidential breath test in the field with the EPAS, via the Cassiopeia® and the magnetic card reader, or via the virtual keyboard and Jot® system on the Cassiopeia®.

#### *Evidential Testing with the Magnetic Card Reader*

Open the *EPAS* case and press the program button on the Cassiopeia®. Next, swipe the subject's driver's license through the magnetic card reader. Verify that all of the data boxes for the subject's information are green.

Next, swipe the operator's card through the magnetic card reader. Verify that all of the operator's data boxes are green.

Enter a violation code, and verify that all of the data boxes are now green.

Tap the "Upload" option on the touch screen, and the data is automatically uploaded to the Alcotest® 7410*Plus*.

The Alcotest® 7410*Plus* powers up and is now ready to conduct an evidential breath test.

The 7410 will start the evidential test sequence by displaying the date:

$$\boxed{\mathsf{nn}}, \boxed{\mathsf{08}} \quad \boxed{\mathsf{dd}}, \boxed{\mathsf{06}} \quad \boxed{\mathsf{'44}}, \boxed{\mathsf{'99}}$$

followed by the time:

$$\boxed{\mathsf{hh}}, \boxed{\mathsf{15}} \quad \boxed{\mathsf{nn}}, \boxed{\mathsf{45}}$$

followed by: $\boxed{- - -}, \boxed{\mathsf{A8L}}$ (Air Blank),

followed by: $\boxed{\mathsf{T}} \boxed{\mathsf{0.00}}$ (Result).

Note: If alcohol is detected by the 7410 in the ambient air or the 7410 has not reached .000 from the previous breath test, the 7410 will automatically perform additional Air Blanks until .000 is displayed.

After a successful Air Blank, the 7410 will display $\boxed{\text{- - -}}$,

then $\boxed{\text{b r 1}}$ (Breath Test Number 1) followed simultaneously by the horn, green "Ready" light.

Instruct the subject to take a deep breath and blow evenly as long as the horn sounds. If the test was successful the result will automatically be displayed: $\boxed{\text{- - -}}$. The unit will proceed to to the second test.

Note: If the test was not successful, EO will be displayed and the test repeated when the green "Ready" light comes on.

For the second breath test $\boxed{\text{b r 2}}$, the above steps will be repeated.

### Evidential Testing with the Virtual Keyboard and Jot®

To conduct an evidential breath test using the virtual keyboard or Jot®, open the case and press the program button on the Cassiopeia®.

Next, tap the first data box for the subject's data, and enter the data using the virtual keyboard or the Jot® system.

Enter all subject and operator data, including a violation code. All of the data boxes should now be green, indicating that data has been successfully entered.

When all subject and operator data has been entered, tap the "Upload" option from the Cassiopeia® touch screen. The data is automatically entered into the Alcotest® 7410$^{Plus}$, which is now ready to conduct an evidential test.

The 7410 will start the evidential test sequence by displaying the date:

$\boxed{\text{nn}},\quad \boxed{\text{08}}\quad \boxed{\text{dd}},\quad \boxed{\text{06}}\quad \boxed{\text{'44}}\quad \boxed{\text{'99}}$

followed by the time:

$$\boxed{hh}, \boxed{15}, \boxed{nn}, \boxed{45}$$

followed by: $\boxed{.---}$, $\boxed{ABL}$ (Air Blank),

followed by: $\boxed{\uparrow}$ $\boxed{.000}$ (Result).

> Note: If alcohol is detected by the 7410 in the ambient air or the 7410 has not reached .000 from the previous breath test, the 7410 will automatically perform additional Air Blanks until .000 is displayed.

After a successful Air Blank, the 7410 will display $\boxed{.---}$,

then $\boxed{br1}$ (Breath Test Number 1) followed simultaneously by the horn, green "Ready" light.

Instruct the subject to take a deep breath and blow evenly as long as the horn sounds. If the test was successful the result will automatically be displayed. After 5 seconds the result will be cleared and the following is displayed: $\boxed{.---}$. The unit will proceed to the second test.

> Note: If the test was not successful, EO will be displayed and the test repeated when the green "Ready" light comes on.

For the second breath test ($\boxed{br2}$), the above steps will be repeated.

**Aborting Test or Subject Refusal**

If the operator wants to abort the test or the subject does not deliver a breath sample within a preset time frame, approx. 45 seconds, after $\boxed{br1}$ or $\boxed{br2}$ is displayed, $\boxed{End}$ will be displayed along with a series of short beeps.

The operator can select by pressing the ON/OFF button once while the beeping continues. An arrow will appear on the display to indicate that END TEST was selected ($\boxed{End}$).

The results of the $\boxed{\text{End}}$ can be printed by following the printing procedures.

If the ON/OFF button is not pressed, the $\boxed{\text{End}}$ will disappear after 5 seconds and the breath test can be administered.

---

Note: the 7410 will continue to go through the above "time out" sequence until a breath test is conducted or $\boxed{\text{End}}$ is selected.

---

Important: If the two Evidential Breath Tests are not within 0.02 gm/210L of each other, the decimal point will flash, and $\boxed{\text{br 3}}$ will be displayed, indicating that a third test is required.

---

Once the test is completed, the 7410 will store the data in its memory.

The test results can be printed at this time by aligning the LCD's (On and Ready lights of the 7410) with the window on the printer.

Press the ON/OFF button of the 7410 two times to turn the unit off, or once to clear the results and get ready for another test.

EXAMPLES OF PRINTOUT

```
YOUR LOCATION HERE
ALCOTEST 7410 PLUS
SERIAL NUMBER:  ARMD-0253

ALCOTEST 7410 PRINTER
SERIAL NUMBER: AREE-0141

MM.DD.YY.  HH:MM
 02 . 24. 00  18:20    ST
SEQUENTIAL TEST # :  00098
****************************************
            SUBJECT:
SURNAME :          KRAPPUR
NAME :               JOHAN
CDL :                 55-67891
DOB :                10-07-1970
         OPERATOR:
LAST:                DEETER
FIRST:               STEVEN
ID-NUMBER :  678-907-2543
AGENCY :             CHP
****************************************

AIR BLANK          0.000 17:36
BREATH TEST 1   0.09   17:37
BREATH TEST 2   0.09   17:41
BREATH TEST 3   .- - - -  - -:- -
    ALL RESULTS IN gm/210L
****************************************

15 MINUTE OBSERVE _____
OPERATOR SIGNATURE:


.................................................

————CUT HERE————
```

Example of Evidential
Breath Test printout.

```
YOUR LOCATION HERE
ALCOTEST 7410 PLUS
SERIAL NUMBER:  ARMD-0253

MM.DD.YY.  HH:MM
 10 . 14. 97  18:20    ST
SEQUENTIAL TEST # :  00075
****************************************
       SCREENING TEST :
AIR BLANK        0.000    09:59
BREATH TEST    0.038    14:37
   ALL RESULTS IN gm/210
****************************************

OPERATOR SIGNATURE:


.................................................
```

Example of Screening Test
printout.

```
YOUR LOCATION HERE
ALCOTEST 7410 PLUS
SERIAL NUMBER:  ARMD-0253

ALCOTEST 7410 PRINTER
SERIAL NUMBER: AREE-0141

MM.DD.YY.  HH:MM
 10 . 14. 97  18:20    DST
SEQUENTIAL TEST # :  00098
****************************************
       ACCURACY TEST
AIR BLANK         0.000   17:36
TEST RESULT     0.090   17:37
   ALL RESULTS IN gm/210L
****************************************

OPERATOR SIGNATURE:

.................................................
```

Example of Accuracy Check
printout.

Trouble Shooting

| FAULT | CAUSE | REMEDY |
|-------|-------|--------|
| Instrument switches off automatically or yellow light is not lit after switching on, or is only faintly lit; the display shows incomplete symbols. | Battery pack is discharged, or battery pack is completely exhausted. Instrument has been left ready for measurement for more than 10 minutes. | Recharge battery pack. |
| "READY" light is not lit after switching on and 10 minute waiting interval has not elapsed. | Instrument Malfunction. | Contact Draeger Safety Customer Support Department. |
| No continuous audible tone when blowing into the instrument. | Instrument not yet ready for measurement. Horn needs replacement (very unusual) or intake is blocked by foreign matter. | Wait until green "READY" light is lit. Contact Draeger Safety, Inc. Customer Support Department. |

| ERROR CODE | CAUSE | REMEDY |
|---|---|---|
| E0 | Test subject is not blowing hard enough or steadily enough. Intake is blocked by foreign matter. Pressure sensor or flow rate suspect. | Ask subject to blow harder or more steadily. Sensor or flow rate must be checked by Draeger Safety, Inc. Technical Department. |
| E1 | RFI present or sensor fault (unusual). | Switch instrument off, change location, and switch back on. If E1 persists, sensor must be inspected by Draeger Safety, Inc. Technical Department. |
| E2 | Instrument does not recognize calibration clip. Cal switch malfunction. | Attach calibration clip correctly before turning on instrument. Cal switch must be replaced by an authorized Service Technician. |
| E3 | Calibration data invalid. Lifetime of sensor reached or cal data malfunction. | Calibrate instrument. Sensor must be replaced or inspected by Draeger Safety. |
| E4 | Improper value was used for calibration. | Calibrate with proper value. |
| E5 | Fault in sampling system (due, most likely, to motor malfunction). | Repeat measurement. If E5 reappears, contact Draeger Safety, Inc. |
| E6 | Instrument Malfunction. | Contact Draeger Safety, Inc. Customer Support Department. |
| E7 | Sensor signal error. | Contact Draeger Safety, Inc. Customer Support Department. |
| Err | Breath test or Accuracy Check is out of limits. | Calibrate instrument. |

Printer

| FAULT | CAUSE | REMEDY |
|-------|-------|--------|
| Not printing although supply voltage is supplied. | Voltage is too low, too high, or wrong polarity. Defective fuse malfunction. | Detach unit from power supply, provide voltage greater than 9.5V/1A and less than 17V/1A. Detach unit from power supply and replace fuse (1A). Contact Draeger Safety Customer Support Department. |
| Although supply voltage is available, paper feed is irregular or printer stops. | Faulty power cord. Power supply inadequate or faulty. Mounting Socket broken. | Replace power cord. Provide voltage greater than 9.5V/1A and less than 17V/1A. Contact Draeger Safety, Inc. Customer Support Department. |

| Message printed | Cause | Remedy |
|-----------------|-------|--------|
| DATA ACCEPTED | Printer received complete new data record. | Normal function message. |
| DATA AVAILABLE | Printer received known data record. | Normal function message. |
| TRANSMISSION ERROR | Incorrect log received. | Position Alcotest® 7410$^{Plus}$ again, or clean transparent window or lenses. |
| BATTERY EMPTY | Memory battery for time and date is empty. | Replace memory batteries (2 x type AA/ 1.5V). |
| HARDWARE ERROR | Hardware error. | Contact Draeger Safety, Inc. Customer Support Department. |

# 5

# INTRODUCTION TO
# BLOOD-ALCOHOL ANALYSIS

## §5.2 Retrograde Extrapolation: Projecting Test Levels Back to Time of Driving

### §5.2.1 The Fallacy of Retrograde Extrapolation

*Page 260. Add at end of first full paragraph:*

In the first cited article, Dubowski also reported variation in *elimination* rates of .001 percent to .08 percent per hour. In another study of subjects who consumed mixed drinks with a meal, researchers found absorption rates ranging from .02 percent to .08 percent per hour; the average was .05 percent. Jones & Neri, 24 Canadian Society of Forensic Sciences Journal 165 (1991).

## §5.3 General Sources of Error

### §5.3.9 Internally Produced Alcohol

*Page 292. Add at end of subsection 5.3.9:*

If the client was taking antacids such as Tums or Rolaids, he may have created a situation in which his body was manufacturing alcohol internally. Scientific literature indicates that antacids change the gastric acidity in the stomach — which can lead to alcohol production by resident bacteria and elevated blood-alcohol readings. Bode, et al., Effects of Cimetidine Treatment on Ethanol Formation in the Human Stomach, 19(6) Scandinavian Journal of Gastroenterology 853 (1984); Ericson, Effects of Antacids on Alcohol's Reaction, 5(5) Alcoholism 28 (1985).

# 6

## BREATH ANALYSIS

### §6.0 The Reliability of Breath-Alcohol Analysis

#### §6.0.1 The Blood-Breath Partition Ratio

**Page 301. Add at end of subsection:**

Confronted with the reality of a legislative/judicial bar to presenting scientific truth as to the partition ratio, counsel should consider turning the new "breath statute" against itself. This can be done by emphasizing the minute amount of breath measured compared to the amount involved in defining the offense. The new statute's definition clearly requires the breath test to be based upon grams of alcohol per 210 liters of breath — a rather voluminous amount. The simple fact is, however, that the lung capacity of human beings is only about four to six liters of breath; the breath machines can capture only about 50 cubic centimeters of this breath for analysis — about 1/20th of one liter. In other words, the machine is measuring a breath sample that is a tiny fraction of the amount relevant to the charge: the statute's 210 liters is about 4200 times more than the sample being analyzed by the machine. Assuming a reading on the machine of .08 percent, this 50 cc breath sample would contain about *one-millionth of a fluid ounce of alcohol.* Is the machine capable of reliably and accurately measuring such an infinitesimal amount? Can the amount of alcohol in 210 liters (the size of an oil drum) be determined from measuring a quantity so tiny that it is invisible to the human eye?

What would be the impact of even the slightest error if magnified 4200 times?

## §6.1   Non-Specific Analysis

*Page 316. Add after second paragraph:*

Note: As is discussed in §6.4.6, Draeger's new Alcotest 7110 incoporates dual technology (infrared and fuel cell) and a new 9.5-micron filter, which will improve specificity. Contrary to claims, however, the non-specificity problem is far from solved. One of the leading figures in breath-alcohol analysis, Professor Dominick A. Labianca, has conducted studies on 9.5-micron filters and has concluded that the ''claim that the most efficient way to avoid the influence of organic compounds in evidential breath testing is the use of the 9.5 micron ethanol absorption band is questionable.'' 404 Journal of Analytical Toxicology 16 (1992):

> Breath-alcohol analyzers operating in the [3.39- and 3.48-micron] wavelength region have been plagued with problems arising from their lack of specificity. . . That lack of specificity is, in part, a consequence of the fact that thousands of organic molecules contain the methyl group, and that the corresponding carbon-hydrogen stretching vibrations of many of these molecules, which can contaminate breath samples, cannot be distinguished from those of ethanol. . . .
>
> While IR [infrared] analyses for breath-alcohol at 9.5-microns would eliminate [some] problems, it would not provide a foolproof solution. Common volatile organic compounds, other than ethanol, which occur, for example, in solvents, perfumes, and food, also contain carbon-oxygen functionality and exhibit IR absorption bands that overlap this wavelength. . .

Draeger has also produced a hand-held version of the Alcotest 7110, the Alcotest 7410 (sometimes referred to as the Breathalyzer 7410; §4.4.1). The California Department of Justice is in the process of replacing all PBT (preliminary breath test) devices and evidential breath testing machines with these PBT-type hand-held units — i.e., the hand-held unit will be offered in court as the primary evidence of blood-alcohol concentration. This development can be expected to spread nationwide.

## §6.3  Additional Sources of Error

### §6.3.8  Ambient Air

*Page 366.  Add at end of subsection:*

The necessity for running a true "air blank" to obtain an arguable accurate breath test result is critical. In fact, however, this step is commonly omitted or done incorrectly — often without the operator's knowledge. Yet, errors in this important step are difficult to detect. The following material, provided to the author by noted forensic toxicologist Mary C. McMurray of Minneapolis, should point counsel in the right directions.*

---

What is an air blank? It isn't a term that you will find in a dictionary, nor is it a term that you can find in an encyclopedia. The term "air blank" is used in the field of breath-alcohol testing, but the meaning of the term varies depending on the source and the context of usage. So what exactly is an air blank?

In 1968, the National Safety Council Committee on Alcohol and Other Drugs developed recommendations for Testing and Training.[1] Included in the recommendations is the requirement for a blank analysis with every test. Unfortunately there is no definition given for the term "blank analysis."

From a pure science perspective, a blank analysis is the analysis (test) of a sample that contains all of the components as the unknown sample(s) *except* the particular compound of interest for which it is being analyzed. Most importantly, the blank must be treated and analyzed in the same manner as the unknown sample(s). The purpose of conducting a blank is to establish whether the sample matrix or the handling of the sample (i.e., the addition

---

*Reprinted with permission.
[1] Committee Handbook 1992, Recommendations of the Ad Hoc Committee on Testing and Training of the Committee on Alcohol and Other Drugs, National Safety Council.

of solvents and/or reagents) has any effect on the detection of the compound in question. A blank analysis is necessary to determine if there is anything in the analytical process that could result in false postive or negative results. A blank analysis is also used for establishing the "background" reading at the time of analysis and is necessary to assure that there is no interference outside of the established parameters.

In blood alcohol analysis a blank would be a blood sample containing no alcohol that is treated in the same manner as the unknown blood samples. The blank-blood samples would have the same preservatives, anticoagulants, internal standards, etc., as the other blood samples and would be handled and analyzed in the same fashion as the blood samples of unknown alcohol concentration. It follows that a blank-breath would be a breath sample that is known to contain no alcohol.

The Federal Register Model Specification for Evidential Breath Alcohol Testers[2] identifies the evaluation process for accuracy and precision for the breath testing devices. One phase of the testing is a blank test, also referred to as testing at 0.0000 BAC. For this testing the analyst is required to abstain from consuming any alcohol for a period of 48 hours prior to the testing and must not smoke for a period of at least 20 minutes prior to testing. The analyst then provides a minimum volume of two liters of his or her own breath into the device being evaluated. The testing parameters require that the systematic error be less than or equal to +/− 0.005 BAC with no single result being greater than 0.005.

In 1971 the Committee on Alcohol and Other Drugs identified the operational standards that should be expected for quantitative breath alcohol analysis and developed guidelines for evaluating evidential breath alcohol testing devices.[3] Among the recommendations is:

> The instrument must be capable of performing a blank analysis on ambient air, free of alcohol and other interfering substances, that yields an apparent alcohol concentration of less than 0.01% W V.-

---

[2] Federal Register, Vol. 58, No. 179, Sept. 17, 1993; Model Specifications for Evidential Breath Alcohol Testers, pages 48705–48710.

[3] Committee Handbook 1992, Recommendations of the Ad Hoc Committee on Quantitative Breath Alcohol Instrumentation of the Committee on Alcohol and Other Drugs, National Safety Council.

Today, the use of an air blank is common in breath-alcohol testing, and all evidential breath-alcohol testing devices have a testing mode for blank analysis. From a scientific perspective, it should be safe to assume that an air blank is an analysis of the ambient air and that if the results of such an analysis are less than a 0.01 g/210L there is no reason to believe that the air or sampling system are contaminated. But are these assumptions correct?

A quick review of the various breath-alcohol testing devices reveals that the air blanks are generally explained in the manufacturer's literature as a check of the ambient air, the sample chamber and/or the fuel cell (if present) to assure that there are no contaminants present that would affect the accuracy of the test results. More than one manufacturer includes information in their operational manual indicating that if the air being drawn into the device is contaminated with alcohol or other detectable substances, some type of "ambient fail" error will be generated alerting the operator. Such statements imply that the purpose of an air-blank analysis is to establish what reading the device shows, at the time of the test, when the ambient air is analyzed.

Precautions do need to be taken to assure that during the air blank analysis the sampling system is not being contaminated. Sources for contamination of an air blank have been traced to used mouthpieces, the breath tube inlet being in close proximity to a heavily contaminated or intoxicated subject, or the recent use of solvents or cleaning compounds in the vicinity of the breath test devices. The installation of the devices should allow for ample air circulation around the vents of the unit, especially the breath exhaust port. The proximity of the breath exhaust port to the inlet of the breath tube can in some cases cause contamination of an air-blank, especially if there is inadequate air circulation around the device.[4]

The concept of an air-blank analysis provides a sense of security that if there is contamination of the sampling system or the

---

[4]While working for the State of Wisconsin, this author was advised, by CMI, to attach a segment of tygon tubing to the exit port of the sample chamber that was long enough to extend under the tabletop. This assured that vapors being purged out of the chamber will not be sucked back into the breath tube where they could potentially contaminate the air blank.

room air the device will indicate such to the operator. The indication being either an alcohol reading on the blank or an audible
and visual display alerting the operator. Interestingly, in evaluating the current evidential instrumentation this hasn't always
proven to be the case. For example, the Intoxilyzer© 5000 uses
the air blank as a purging system, then, using the analysis of the
ambient air sample at the end of the purge, arbitrarily sets zero.
A system such as this will never print a numeric result for an air
blank that is greater than 0.000 g/210L regardless of how much
alcohol or other contamination is in the sampling system[5] The
purpose for performing a blank analysis is totally lost with this
type of a system as there is no way of determining if there is any
contamination of the air or sampling system that would affect the
accuracy of the test results.

The setting of a new "zero" with each and every air blank
can produce some very interesting results. Obviously the recommendation for a blank analysis with every evidential test cannot
be intended to mean the test subject's own breath in an alcohol-
free state. So what is the source of the blank analysis that should
accompany every evidential breath test? Perhaps the breath test
operator could be used as a source for a blank-breath sample —
assuming there is no alcohol, or other interfering substances, on
his or her breath. Instead it was, somehow and somewhere, decided that room air can serve as the blank. It seems logical to
assume that, since room air is inhaled then exhaled as breath, the
ambient air can be used as a source for the blank analysis. It also
seems logical to assume that, in most cases, room air is alcohol
free.

If there is alcohol in the sampling system blank the Intoxily-
zer© will "see" that amount of alcohol as zero — and then sub-
tract that amount of alcohol from the next sample. The result is
not accuate if it is reading too low. An instrument that cannot
detect the very substance that it is supposed to be measuring during an air blank does not assure accuracy.

Some people will argue that the low reading benefits the test
subject. So who cares? If the claim is scientifically accurate and
the results are reliable, you should care. Poor precision of test

---

[5] For more information refer to Law and Science DWI Journal, Vol. 11, No.
6, June 1996 and Vol. 11, No. 7, July 1996.

results can be masked by the floating zero. The arbitrary setting of zero with each air blank can result in what appears to be a 0.02 correlation between two samples or it can mask a correlation and make it appear that two samples are not in agreement. Unfortunately there is no way that a breath test operator will ever know if this is occurring at any given time.

In the August 1994 update to the Omnibus Rules[6] it was noted in the discussion that the main point of an air blank is to ensure that the testing device is a "clean slate" and is unaffected by any alcohol from previous tests or other sources.[7] The Omnibus Rules require the results of an air blank prior to a test to be 0.00 g/210L or the testing is not to be continued on that device. If an air blank preceding a test is not 0.00 the test is considered invalid. The arbitrary establishment of "zero" on each air blank assures that the requirement for a 0.00 g/210L will always be satisfied.

The Department of Transportation regulations for the Omnibus Employee Testing Act[8] definitions for breath alcohol testing in 49 CFR Part 40 includes:

> Air blank: A reading by an EBT of ambient air containing no alcohol. (In EBTs using gas chromatography technology, a reading of the device's internal standard.)[9]

The addition of the use of a device's internal standard in doing a blank check is quite interesting. It is a modification of the concept of an air blank so that an air sample is no longer necessary for the blank analysis. The analysis of blank-breath samples were used to demonstrate that the device does not create false positive or negative results — thus assuring some level of accuracy at the lower limits of detection under laboratory conditons. The air blanks have been used to purge the sampling system followed by an analysis of the ambient air samples — establishing the baseline value for the test device at that point in time. An analysis to assure

---

[6] Federal Register, Vol. 59, No. 160, Aug. 19, 1994. 49 CFR Part 40 Final Rule, page 42999.

[7] Federal Register, Vol. 59, No. 31, Feb. 15, 1994. 49 CFR Part 40 Rules and Regulations, pages 7340–7366. Federal Register, Vol. 59, No. 160, Aug. 19, 1994. 49 CFR Part 40 Final Rule, pages 42996–43019.

[8] Federal Register, Vol. 59, Feb. 15, 1994. 49 CFR Part 40 Rules and Regulations, 7340–7366

[9] EBT is an Evidential Breath Test device.

that there are no contaminants that would affect the accuracy of the test result.

Today a blank analysis means the blank checked itself and is reading 0.00 g/210L. What does such a check show? The blank sample (sometimes referred to as a system blank) is not necessarily a sample. It can be a reading generated by the testing device to show what the sampling system registers at the moment. If the system blank is designed to provide a true reading of what is present in the sampling system then, it can be used to show the baseline or background value. However, if the device simply blanks out the background, a random analytical error is introduced that cannot be measured.

It appears that the air blank can be anything the instrument manufacturer wants it to be without concern for scientific credibility. The air-blank measurement in some cases does not even serve the purpose claimed by the manufacturer. Apparently the efforts of the manufacturer are to placate the breath test governing bodies.

## §6.4　The Machines

*Page 381. Add at end of section:*

Counsel confronted with a breath machine — evidential or PBT (see §4.4) — not commonly encountered should check to see whether it is an *approved* device. Most jurisdictions require any breath-testing equipment to be reviewed and approved by appropriate governmental agencies. Such machines are usually included on a list of "conforming" devices maintained by the state's regulatory agency. In most cases, the agency simply adopts the federal National Highway Traffic Safety Administration's "Conforming Products List" — a list that is periodically updated as some instruments are added while others are discontinued. Any breath tests conducted with an unapproved machine should, of course, be subject to a pretrial motion to suppress.

Counsel should be aware that law enforcement agencies in some states *modify* machines that are on the Conforming Products List. The modifications may be made by the manufacturers at the agency's request, or they may be made by the agencies themselves. It is important to understand that *such modifications create a different device* — and thus one no longer on the list of approved instruments.

The following is the latest available list of conforming breath-testing products, taken from the *Federal Register,* Vol. 65, No. 141, p. 45419 (July 21, 2000):

---

DEPARTMENT OF TRANSPORTATION: National Highway Traffic Safety Administration. [Docket No. NHTSA-00–7570] Highway Safety Programs; Model Specifications for Devices to Measure Breath Alcohol

AGENCY: National Highway Traffic Safety Administration, DOT.

ACTION: Notice.

SUMMARY: This notice amends the Conforming Products List for instruments that conform to the Model Specifications for Evidential Breath Testing Devices (58 FR 48705).

EFFECTIVE DATE: July 21, 2000.

FOR FURTHER INFORMATION CONTACT: Dr. James F. Frank, Office of Traffic Injury Control Programs, Impaired Driving Division (NTS-11), National Highway Traffic Safety Administration, 400 Seventh Street, S.W., Washington, D.C. 20590; Telephone: (202) 366-5593.

SUPPLEMENTARY INFORMATION: On November 5, 1973, the National Highway Traffic Safety Administration (NHTSA) published the Standards for Devices to Measure Breath Alcohol (38 FR 30459). A Qualified Products List of Evidential Breath Measurement Devices comprised of instruments that met this standard was first issued on November 21, 1974 (39 FR 41399).

On December 14, 1984 (49 FR 48854), NHTSA converted this standard to Model Specifications for Evidential Breath Testing Devices, and published a Conforming Products List (CPL) of instruments that were found to conform to the Model Specifications as Appendix D to that notice (49 FR 48864).

On September 17, 1993, NHTSA published a notice (58 FR 48705) to amend the Model Specifications. The notice changed the alcohol concentration levels at which instruments are evaluated, from 0.000, 0.050, 0.101, and 0.151 BAC, to 0.000, 0.020, 0.040, 0.080, and 0.160 BAC; added a test for the presence of acetone; and expanded the definition of alcohol to include other low molecular weight alcohols including methyl or isopropyl. On June 4, 1999, the most recent amendment to the Conforming Products List (CPL) was published (64 FR 30097), identifying those instruments found to conform with the Model Specifications.

Since the last publication of the CPL, two (2) instruments have been evaluated and found to meet the model specifications, as amended on September 17, 1993, for mobile and non-mobile use. They are: (1) Intoxilyzer 400PA manufactured by CMI, Inc. of Owensboro, KY. This device is a hand-held breath tester with a fuel cell alcohol sensor; (2) Alco Sensor IV-XL manufactured by Intoximeters, Inc. of St. Louis, MO. This device is a hand-held breath tester with a fuel cell alcohol sensor that is microprocessor controlled. It is designed to minimize operator involvement in performing the test and processing the test data.

The CPL has been amended to add these two instruments to the list.

In accordance with the foregoing, the CPL is therefore amended, as set forth below.

**Conforming Products List of Evidential Breath Measurement Devices**

| Manufacturer and model | Mobile | Nonmobile |
|---|:---:|:---:|
| Alcohol Countermeasure Systems Corp., Mississauga, Ontario, Canada: | | |
| Alert J3AD* | X | X |
| PBA3000C | X | X |
| BAC Systems, Inc., Ontario, Canada: Breath Analysis Computer* | X | X |
| CAMEC Ltd., North Shields, Tyne and Ware, England: IR Breath Analyzer* | X | X |

*Instruments marked with an asterisk (*) meet the Model Specifications detailed in 49 FR 48854) (December 14, 1984), (*i.e.* instruments tested at 0.000, 0.050, 0.101, and 0.151 BAC.) Instruments not marked with an asterisk meet the Model Specifications detailed in 58 FR 48705 (September 17, 1993), and were tested at BACs = 0.000, 0.020, 0.040, 0,080, and 0.160. All instruments that meet the Model Specifications currently in effect (dated September 17, 1993) also meet the Model Specifications for Screening Devices to Measure Alcohol in Bodily Fluids.

| Manufacturer and model | Mobile | Nonmobile |
|---|---|---|
| CMI, Inc., Owensboro, KY: | | |
| Intoxilyzer Model: | | |
| 200 | X | X |
| 200D | X | X |
| 300 | X | X |
| 400 | X | X |
| 400PA | X | X |
| 1400 | X | X |
| 4011* | X | X |
| 4011A* | X | X |
| 4011AS* | X | X |
| 4011AS-A* | X | X |
| 4011AS-AQ* | X | X |
| 4011 AW* | X | X |
| 4011A27-10100* | X | X |
| 4011A27-10100 with filter* | X | X |
| 5000 | X | X |
| 5000 (w/Cal. Vapor Re-Circ.) | X | X |
| 5000 (w ⅜″ ID Hose option) | X | X |
| 5000CD | X | X |
| 5000CD/FG5 | X | X |
| 5000EN | X | X |
| 5000 (CAL DOJ) | X | X |
| 5000VA | X | X |
| PAC 1200* | X | X |
| S-D2 | X | X |
| Decator Electronics, Decator, IL: Alco-Tector | | |
| model 500* | — | X |
| Draeger Safety, Inc., Durango, CO: | | |
| Alcotest Model: | | |
| 7010* | X | X |
| 7110* | X | X |
| 7110MKIII | X | X |
| 7110MKIII-C | X | X |
| 7410 | X | X |
| 7410Plus | X | X |
| Breathalyzer Model: | | |
| 900* | X | X |
| 900A* | X | X |
| 900BG* | X | X |
| 7410 | X | X |
| 7410-II | X | X |

| Manufacturer and model | Mobile | Nonmobile |
|---|---|---|
| Gall's Inc., Lexington, KY: Alcohol Detection System-A.D.S. 500 | X | X |
| Intoximeters, Inc., St. Louis, MO: | | |
| Photo Electric Intoximeter* | — | X |
| GC Intoximeter MK II* | X | X |
| GC Intoximeter MK IV* | X | X |
| Auto Intoximeter* | X | X |
| Intoximeter Model: | | |
| 3000* | X | X |
| 3000 (rev B1)* | X | X |
| 3000 (rev B2)* | X | X |
| 3000 (rev B2A)* | X | X |
| 3000 (rev B2A) w/FM option* | X | X |
| 3000 (Fuel Cell)* | X | X |
| 3000 D* | X | X |
| 3000 DFC* | X | X |
| Alcomonitor | — | X |
| Alcomonitor CC | X | — |
| Alco-Sensor III | X | X |
| Alco-Sensor IV | X | X |
| Alco-Sensor IV-XL | X | X |
| Alco-Sensor AZ | X | X |
| RBT-AZ | X | X |
| RBT III | X | X |
| RBT III-A | X | X |
| RBT IV | X | X |
| RBT IV with CEM (cell enhancement module) | X | X |
| Intox EC/IR | X | X |
| Portable Intox EC/IR | X | X |
| Komyo Kitagawa, Kogyo, K.K.: | | |
| Alcolyzer DPA-2* | X | X |
| Breath Alcohol Meter PAM 101B* | X | X |
| Lifeloc Technologies, Inc., (formerly Lifeloc, Inc.), Wheat Ridge, CO: | | |
| PBA 3000B | X | X |
| PBA 3000-P* | X | X |
| PBA 3000C | X | X |
| Alcohol Data Sensor | X | X |
| Phoenix | X | X |

| Manufacturer and model | Mobile | Nonmobile |
|---|:---:|:---:|
| Lion Laboratories, Ltd., Cardiff, Wales, UK: | | |
| Alcolmeter Model: | | |
| 300 | X | X |
| 400 | X | X |
| AE-D1* | X | X |
| SE-2* | X | X |
| EBA* | X | X |
| Auto-Alcolmeter* | X | — |
| Intoxilyzer Model: | | |
| 200 | X | X |
| 200D | X | X |
| 1400 | X | X |
| 5000 CD/FG5 | X | X |
| 5000 EN | X | X |
| Luckey Laboratories, San Bernardino, CA: | | |
| Alco-Analyzer Model: | | |
| 1000* | — | X |
| 2000 | X | — |
| National Draeger, Inc., Durango, CO: | | |
| Alcotest Model: | | |
| 7010* | X | X |
| 7110* | X | X |
| 7110 MKIII | X | X |
| 7110 MKIII-C | X | X |
| 7410 | X | X |
| 7410Plus | X | X |
| Breathalyzer Model: | | |
| 900* | X | X |
| 900A* | X | X |
| 900BG* | X | X |
| 7410 | X | X |
| 7410-II | X | X |
| National Patent Analytical Systems, Inc., Mansfield, OH: | | |
| BAC DataMaster (with or without the Delta-1 accessory | X | X |
| BAC Verifier Datamaster (with or without the Delta-1 accessory) | X | X |
| DataMaster cdm (with or without the Delta-1 accessory) | X | X |

| Manufacturer and model | Mobile | Nonmobile |
|---|:---:|:---:|
| Omicron Systems, Palo Alto, CA: | | |
| Intoxilyzer Model: | | |
| 4011* | X | X |
| 4011AW* | X | X |
| Plus 4 Engineering, Minturn, CO: 5000 Plus4* | X | X |
| Seres, Paris, France: | | |
| Alco Master | X | X |
| Alcopro | X | X |
| Siemans-Allis, Cherry Hill, NJ: | | |
| Alcomat* | X | X |
| Alcomat F* | X | X |
| Smith and Wesson Electronics, Springfield, MA: | | |
| Breathalyzer Model: | | |
| 900* | X | X |
| 900A* | X | X |
| 1000* | X | X |
| 2000* | X | X |
| 2000 (non-Humidity Sensor)* | X | X |
| Sound-Off, Inc., Hudsonville, MI: | | |
| AlcoData | X | X |
| Seres Alco Master | X | X |
| Seres Alcopro | X | X |
| Stephenson Corp.: Breathalyzer 900* | X | X |
| U.S. Alcohol Testing, Inc./Protection Devices, Inc., Rancho Cucamonga, CA: | | |
| Alco-Analyzer 1000 | — | X |
| Alco-Analyzer 2000 | — | X |
| Alco-Analyzer 2100 | X | X |
| Verax Systems, Inc., Fairport, NY: | | |
| BAC Verifier* | X | X |
| BAC Verifier Datamaster | X | X |
| BAC Verifier Datamaster II* | X | X |

(23 U.S.C. 402; delegations of authority at 49 CFR 1.50 and 501.1)

Issued on: February 24, 1998.
James L. Nichols,
Acting Associate Administrator for Traffic Safety Programs.
[FR Doc. 98-5093 Filed 2-26-98; 8:45 a.m.]
BILLING CODE 4910-59-P

## §6.4.2 BAC DataMaster

*Page 435. Add at end of fact #6:*

Correction: The DataMaster continues to be manufactured by National Patent.

## §6.4.6 Alcotest 7110

*Page 507. Add after* SAFEGUARD 4 *paragraph:*

ERROR INDICATORS — The Alcotest 7110 is equipped with various error analysis features in the event of a systematic problem. In such a case, the display and printer will indicate the error condition according to the following chart (for example: ERROR [081] INTERFACT-SYS>).

| Error Code | Error name: | Potential reason for error: |
|---|---|---|
| 002 | MAIN-SYSTEM, EEPROM memory | Defective memory cell |
| 003 | MAIN-SYSTEM, RAM memory | Defective memory cell |
| Error Code | Error name: | Potential reason for error: |
| 004 | MAIN-SYSTEM, External RAM memory | Defective memory cell |
| 008 | MAIN-SYSTEM, Battery for memory | Discharged battery |
| 009 | MAIN-SYSTEM, Power supply | 12 VDC insufficient. Turn instrument off and on again. |
| 023 | IR-SYSTEM, Source oscillator | Frequency too low |
| 031 | EC-SYSTEM, EC-signal | Incorrect voltage, or early warning that the fuel cell may need to be replaced |
| 032 | EC-SYSTEM, Sampling system | Motor, pump, relay |
| 035 | EC-SYSTEM, EC-peak signal | Signal peak not found |
| 041 | FLOW-SYSTEM, Flow sensor | Short or interrupted circuit |
| 043 | FLOW-SYSTEM, Purge | Insufficient flow for air blank. Check to see that back of unit is not obstructed. |

| 051 | PRESSURE-SYSTEM, Pressure sensor | Short or interrupted circuit |
| 071 | HEATER-SYSTEM, NTC for cuvette | Short or interrupted circuit |
| 072 | HEATER-SYSTEM, NTC for breath hose | Short or interrupted circuit |
| 075 | HEATER-SYSTEM, Temperature(s) | Cuvette-, breath hose-heater malfunctioning |
| 081 | INTERFACE-SYSTEM, Printer | No printer commands |
| 084 | INTERFACE-SYSTEM, Function-key | Unacceptable voltage |
| 101 | CALIBRATION, IR-system | Unacceptable adjustment |
| 112 | CALIBRATION, Calibration data | Lost data in EEPROM |
| 113 | CALIBRATION, Configuration | System parameters incorrect |

*Page 515.  Add after chart:*

The chart "Selected Compounds with C-O Stretching Vibrations that Absorb in the 9–10 micron Region" was created by Professor Dominick A. Labianca, Ph.D., and may be cited as: Labianca, D.A., How Specific for Ethanol Is Breath-Alcohol Analysis Based on Absorption of IR Radiation at 9.5 microns?, 16 Journal of Analytical Toxicology 404 (1992).

*Page 515.  Add new subsection:*

### §6.4.7   Intoximeter EC/IR

Intoximeter, Inc.'s Intoximeter EC/IR (standing for electrochemical/infrared) is a relatively new breath alcohol machine, replacing the manufacturer's older model, the Intoximeter 3000. The primary difference between the two devices is that the EC/IR uses fuel cell and infrared analysis, where the 3000 utilized gas chromatography. In this respect it is similar to Draeger's Alcotest 7110 (see §6.4.6). The dual technology gives the machine improved specificity as to ethanol (see §6.1), but the device remains prone to most of the other problems inherent in breath-alcohol analysis discussed elsewhere — mouth alcohol, radio frequency interference, retrograde extrapolation, partition ratio variance, etc.

Note: The author has received reports from attorneys in some states that have recently adopted the EC/IR as an evidentiary machine. They indicate that the RFI (radio frequency interence) detector and the slope (mouth alcohol) detector have been turned off. One attorney was advised by the state's senior chemist that this was suggested by the manufacturer to facilitate proper use of the machine. To determine whether these critical detectors have been disconnected in a given machine, seek through discovery a printout of the internal operating standards (easily obtainable with the machine's F11 key).

Note also: As with some other breath testing machines (see §13.3.5), Intoximeter's EC/IR has a limited manufacturer's warranty — for only one year and with no warranty as to software.

The following material taken from the Los Angeles Police Department's "Intox EC/IR Administrator's Manual," is largely reproduced from the manufacturer's manual. Counsel should consider an officer's administration of the test in light of the recommended procedures set forth in the manual. The material also offers possibilities for exploring the officer's lack of knowledge of the machine's theory and operation.

## TECHNICAL SPECIFICATIONS

### Measurement Range

0.000 to 0.400 grams of ethanol/210 liters of breath

### Accuracy and Precision

The Intox EC/IR meets or exceeds all US Department of Transportation specifications for the accuracy and precision of alcohol breath testing instruments. The measurement system is specific to ethyl, methyl, and isopropyl alcohols; it does not respond to other hydrocarbons found naturally in the breath.

The Intox EC/IR is accurate to within 0.003 at 0.100 BrAC.

### Internal Clock and Calendar

The internal clock, with or without external power, is accurate to ±1 minute per month.

## Keyboard

101-key, AT-compatible keyboard.

## Display

The Intox EC/IR display is two line by twenty character vacuum fluorescent display. The display is:

- highly reliable — rated for a lifetime of 50,000 hours
- very bright — 685 cd/m$^2$ (or 200 f-L)
- has low power consumption
- supports a large international character set

## Printer

The Intox EC/IR incorporates a high performance thermal printer that provides:

- Printing speed 7.5 lines per second
- 150 dots/inch resolution
- Integrated paper handling system requires no threading; changing the paper roll takes seconds and there are no paper jams
- Multiple test modes, including compressed, double width and height, bold and reverse image
- Large international character set

## Optional External Printer

The Intox EC/IR can print to most IBM PC-compatible printers with a Centronics parallel interface via the 25-pin connector on the instrument's rear panel.

## Modem

The Intox EC/IR can communicate via a built-in Hayes-compatible 2400 baud modem. A built-in Hayes-compatible 9600 baud modem is optional.

## I/O

2 - RS-232 serial communications ports
1 - parallel port

### Electrical

90 to 250 VAC, 47 to 63 Hz, approximaely 65 watts power consumption
12 VDC operation with optional inverter

### Mechanical

Desktop model

Height: 7 in. (178 mm)
Width: 17 3/4 in. (451 mm)
Depth: 18 in. (457 mm)
Weight: 22 lb. (10 kg)

Portable model

Height: 7 in. (178 mm)
Width: 14 in. (356 mm)
Depth: 18 in. (457 mm)
Weight (with tank): 30 lb. (14 kg)

## SUBJECT TESTS

### LOS ANGELES POLICE DEPARTMENT PROTOCOL

The following procedures illustrate testing using the Los Angeles Police Department protocol. The Los Angeles Police Department protocol is a two-test protocol with a conditional third test preceded by a series of questions about the subject and operator.

### Conducting a Subject Test Using the Los Angeles Police Department

Once the system has been turned on and the warm-up cycle completed the display will be in the scrolling mode. Follow the steps below noting the display, keyboard entry, and explanation at each step. Note: Always use a new originally packaged mouth piece for each subject test. Use care when opening the mouthpiece package. Residual pieces of plastic wrap may cling to the mouthpiece which may get blown into the sample assembly causing restriction and possible blockage.

| DISPLAY | KEYBOARD ENTRY | EXPLANATION |
|---|---|---|
| Normal Scrolling Mode<br>INTOX EC/IR<br>TEST SITE A49<br>SERIAL NO. 01780<br>13:59 05/08/95<br>PRESS ENTER TO START<br>SUBJECT TEST | Press the Enter key. | The Enter key starts the test. |
| SUBJECT TEST | Information only. No data entry required. | |
| SUBJECT NAME: JOHN T. SMITH | Enter the test subject's name. John T. Smth. | Entry may be up to 20 characters. |
| OPERATOR SERIAL #: 153761 | Enter the Operator's serial #. 153761 | Entry may be up 6 numeric characters. |
| OPERATOR ASSIGNMENT: | Enter the Operator's assignment. | Entry may be up to 20 characters. |
| 15 MIN OBSERVED BY: | Enter the serial # of the person who observed the subject during the 15 minute waiting period. | Entry may be up to 6 numeric characters. |
| VERIFY DATA (Y/N)? N | Enter Y to review or edit the previously entered data, or press the Enter key to continue. | Allows the operator to review or edit the previously entered data and correct any errors. |
| CHECKING SYSTEM | Information only. No data entry required. | The instrument is performing an internal electronic system check. |
| PURGING | Information only. No data entry required. | The Intox EC/IR is purging the breath path with ambient air. |
| BLANK CHECK | Information only. No data entry required. | The instrument will flush the breath path with room air for approximately 30 seconds. A sample of this air is analyzed. If the result is .000, the Standard Check is initiated. If the result is >.000 a second purge is done. If a third blank result is >.000 the test is aborted. |
| BLANK .000 | Information only. No data entry required. | The instrument diplays the result of the blank check. |

| DISPLAY | KEYBOARD ENTRY | EXPLANATION |
|---|---|---|
| PLEASE BLOW<br>************* | If the subject refuses to submit a breath sample press the R key. The test will be aborted and the printer will print all of the subject data followed by "TEST REFUSED." | Instruct the subject to take a deep breath and blow into the mouth piece as steadily and as long as possible. Flow and volume will be indicated by the * characters.<br><br>The test subject is allowed 4 minutes to provide a valid sample. If he/she fails to do so, the test will be treated as a refusal. |
| EVALUATING SAMPLE | Information only. No data entry required. | The Intox EC/IR is evaluating the sample. |
| SUBJECT .00 | Information only. No data entry required. | The instrument displays the result of the subject test. |
| PURGING | Information only. No data entry required. | The Intox EC/IR is purging the breath path with ambient air. |
| BLANK CHECK | Information only. No data entry required. | The instrument will flush the breath path with room air for approximately 30 seconds. A sample of this air is analyzed. If the result is .000, the Standard Check is initiated. If the result is >.000 a second purge is done. If a third blank result is >.000 the test is aborted. |
| BLANK .000 | Information only. No data entry required. | The instrument displays the result of the Blank Check. |
| PLEASE BLOW<br>********* | If the subject refuses to submit a breath sample press the R key. The test will be aborted and the printer will print all of the subject data followed by "TEST REFUSED." | Instruct the subject to take a deep breath and blow into the mouth piece as steadily and as long as possible. Flow and volume will be indicated by the * characters.<br><br>The test subject is allowed 4 minutes to provide a valid sample. Failure is treated as a refusal. |
| EVALUATING SAMPLE | Information only. No data entry required. | The Intox EC/IR is evaluating the sample. |

| DISPLAY | KEYBOARD ENTRY | EXPLANATION |
|---|---|---|
| SUBJECT .00 | Information only. No data entry required. | The instrument displays the result of the Subject test. |
| | If the result of the two subject tests differ by more than .02, a third test will be run and reported in the printout. | Printer now prints the test results as shown below: |

```
Intox EC/IR
SUBJECT TEST
S/N: 01780
Location:
TEST SITE A49
Test Date: 01/12/98
Test Time: 12:42

Subject's Name:
John T. Smith
Operator Serial #:
A53242
Operator Assignment:
15 Minimum Observed
By:
476432
TEST      g/2101 Time
Diagnostic Check ok

BLK     .00   02:41
SUBJ    .00   02:42
BLK     .00   02:43
SUBJ    .00   02:44
```

| DISPLAY | KEYBOARD ENTRY | EXPLANATION |
|---|---|---|
| PRINT ANOTHER COPY? (Y/N) N | Enter Y to print another copy of the test result or the Enter key to continue. | Multiple copies of the Subject Test printout can be obtained at this point. |
| PURGING | Information only. No data entry required. | The Intox EC/IR is purging the breath path with ambient air. |
| Normal Scrolling Mode | Information only. No data entry required. | The instrument returns to the Normal Scrolling Mode. |

## DOT PROTOCOL

The following procedures illustrate testing using the DOT protocol. The DOT protocol involves a Screening Test followed by a conditional Confirmation Test. The Intox EC/IR will instruct the Operator on the proper sequence of steps needed to perform a DOT protocol alcohol test.

## Conducting A Subject Test Using DOT Protocol

Follow the steps below noting the display, keyboard entry, and explanation at each step.

| DISPLAY | KEYBOARD ENTRY | EXPLANATION |
|---|---|---|
| Normal Scrolling Mode<br><br>INTOX EC/IR<br>TEST SITE A49<br>S/N 01780<br>13:59 05/08/95<br>PRESS ENTER TO START<br>DOT<br>SUBJECT TEST | Press the Enter key. | The Enter key starts the test. |
| PASSWORD **** | Enter your password then press the Enter key. | This function requires an Operator level or higher password. |
| *RUN SCHEDULED ACC CHECK (Y/N)? Y* | Press the Enter key to initiate the scheduled accuracy check. | This message will only appear before the first test of a given day if a scheduled accuracy check is required. The frequency of scheduled accuracy checks is set under the F10 key. |
| *SUBJECT TEST DISABLED* | After displaying this message for approximately 5 seconds, the Intox EC/IR will return to scrolling mode. | If a required accuracy check has not been completed, one must be completed successfully before the Intox EC/IR will allow another test to be run. |
| SCREEN OR CONFIRM (S/C)? S | Press the Enter key to initiate a Screen Test. Press C and the Enter key for a Confirmation Test. | |

THE FOLLOWING SERIES OF STEPS WILL OCCUR IN EITHER A SCREEN TEST OR A CONFIRMATION ONLY TEST.

| STEP 1 ON FORM COMPLETED (Y/N)? Y | Complete Step 1 on the DOT test form and then press the Enter key to continue. | |
|---|---|---|

| DISPLAY | KEYBOARD ENTRY | EXPLANATION |
|---|---|---|
| DATE: MON 12 JUN 95 OK (Y/N)? Y | If the time is correct press the enter key to continue. If the time is incorrect, Type N and the Enter key. | If the Operator answers N to this question the Intox EC/IR exits the test sequence and instructs the Operator that a Key Operator must reset the date. |
| TIME: 14:43 OK (Y/N)? Y | If the time is correct press the enter key to continue. If the time is incorrect, Type N and the Enter key. | If the Operator answers N to this question the Intox EC/IR exits the test sequence and instructs the Operator that a Key Operator must reset the date. |
| ENTER BAT NAME/ID: BOB JONES | Enter the BAT's name. Bob Jones | Entry may be up to 20 characters. |
| EMPLOYEE FIRST NAME: JOHN | Enter the subject's first name. John | Entry may be up to 20 characters. |
| EMPLOYEE MIDDLE I: T | Enter the subject's middle initial. T | Entry must be 1 character. |
| EMPLOYEE LAST NAME: SMITH | Enter the subject's last name. Smith | Entry may be up to 20 characters. |
| EMPLOYEE ID: 453 6125 23 | Enter the subject's ID 453 6125 23 | Entry may be up to 20 characters. |
| COMPANY ID: ABC145 | Enter the ID of the subject's employer ABC145 | Entry may be up to 20 characters. |
| COMPANY NAME: ABC CORPORATION | Enter the name of the subject's employer. ABC CORPORATION | Entry may be up to 20 characters. |
| REASON FOR TEST (1-6) PRE-EMPLOYMENT | Type a digit from 1 to 6 to enter the DOT reason for test. | 1 Pre-employment 2 Random 3 Suspicion/cause 4 Post-accident 5 Return to duty 6 Follow-up |
| VERIFY DATA (Y/N)? N | Enter Y or N. N | Entering Y allows the operator to review and/or edit the previous entries and correct any errors. |
| EXPLAIN TEST PROC. THEN PRESS ENTER | Explain the test procedure to the subject and then press the Enter key to continue. | |

| DISPLAY | KEYBOARD ENTRY | EXPLANATION |
|---|---|---|
| STEP 2 ON FORM COMPLETED (Y/N)? Y | Complete Step 2 in the DOT test form and then press the Enter key to continue. | |
| INSERT MOUTHPIECE THEN ENTER | Insert the mouthpiece into the breath tube and then press the Enter key. | The Operator should put the mouthpiece into the breath tube at this time so that the Intox EC/IR's purge/blank procedure will insure that the mouthpiece is not contaminated with alcohol. |

THE FOLLOWING SERIES OF STEPS WILL OCCUR ONLY IF A SCREEN TEST IS BEING RUN.

| | | |
|---|---|---|
| SCREEN #: 950612091 OBSERVED (Y/N)? Y | Note the test number and then press the Enter key to continue. | Display shows the test number until the Enter key is pressed. The format is YYMMDDXXX where XXX is the test number. |
| CHECKING SYSTEM | Information only. No data entry required. | The instrument is performing self-diagnostic checks. |
| PURGING | Information only. No data entry required. | The instument is purging the sample path with ambient air. |
| BLOW UNTIL BEEP \*\*\*\*\*\*\*\*\* TIME LEFT: 02:56 | If the subject refuses to submit a breath sample press the R key. The test will be aborted and the printer will print all of the subject data followed by "TEST REFUSED." If the timer expires, the message TEST REFUSED (Y/N)? will be displayed. | Instruct the subject to take a deep breath and blow into the mouthpiece as steadily and as long as possible. Flow and volume will be indicated by the * characters. Typing Shift-M will force a manual sample (See Breath Sample Volume section of Operating Principles). |
| EVALUATING SAMPLE then RESULT 0.044  14:45 | Information only. No data entry required. | The Intox EC/IR is evaluating the sample. Printer now prints the test results as shown below: |

| DISPLAY | KEYBOARD ENTRY | EXPLANATION |
|---|---|---|

PRINT ANOTHER COPY?
(Y/N)? Y

Press Y and the Enter key
for another copy or press
the Enter key to continue.

Screening Test
Intox EC/IR
S/N: 01780
Location:
TEST SITE A49
Date: Mon 12 Jun 95
Time: 14:45

Test #: 950612091

Employee ID:
453 6125 23

|  | VALUE (g/2101) | TIME |
|---|---|---|
| Result | 0.044 | 14:45 |

---

| DISPLAY | KEYBOARD ENTRY | EXPLANATION |
|---|---|---|
| RESULT 0.044    14:45<br>OBSERVED (Y/N)? Y | After showing the subject<br>the results, press Enter. |  |
| ATTACH PRINTOUT TO<br>FORM, PRESS ENTER | Attach the printout to the<br>DOT alcohol test form<br>then press enter to<br>continue. |  |

IF THE RESULT OF THE SCREEN TEST IS LESS THAN .020 THEN THE TEST
SEQUENCE WILL TERMINATE WITH THE FOLLOWING STEPS:

| DISPLAY | KEYBOARD ENTRY | EXPLANATION |
|---|---|---|
| COMPLETE FORM STEP<br>3 THEN PRESS ENTER | Complete Step 3 on the<br>DOT test form and then<br>press the Enter key to<br>continue. |  |
| COMPLETE FORM STEP<br>4 THEN PRESS ENTER | Complete Step 4 on the<br>DOT test form and then<br>press the Enter key to<br>continue. |  |
| PURGING | Information only. No data<br>entry required. | Instrument is purging the<br>breath path with ambient<br>air. |
| Normal Scrolling Mode | Information only. No data<br>entry required. | The instrument returns to<br>Normal Scrolling Mode. |

IF THE RESULT OF THE SCREEN TEST IS GREATER THAN .020 THEN THE TEST
SEQUENCE WILL CONTINUE WITH THE FOLLOWING STEPS:

| DISPLAY | KEYBOARD ENTRY | EXPLANATION |
|---|---|---|
| DO CONFIRMATION TEST<br><br>15 MINUTE WAIT 13:24<br>REMOVE MOUTHPIECE<br>THEN PRESS ENTER | Remove the mouthpiece from the breath tube and then press the Enter key. | The Intox EC/IR will beep as a reminder to remove the mouthpiece until the Enter key is pressed. After the Enter key is pressed, only the timer portion of the message will appear on the screen.<br><br>When there is less than 1 minute left on the timer the Intox EC/IR will begin beeping. |
| 15 MINUTE WAIT 13:24 | | After the 15 minute wait the Operator must begin the Confirmation test within 15 minutes. |

THE FOLLOWING SERIES OF STEPS WILL OCCUR FOR A CONFIRMATION TEST AS A CONFIRMATION ONLY TEST OR AS A CONFIRMATION TEST FOLLOWING A POSITIVE SCREENING TEST.

| DISPLAY | KEYBOARD ENTRY | EXPLANATION |
|---|---|---|
| CONFIRMATION TEST INSERT NEW MOUTHPIECE THEN PRESS ENTER | Insert the mouthpiece into the breath tube and then press the Enter key. | The Operator should put the mouthpiece into the breath tube at this time so that the Intox EC/IR's purge/blank procedure will insure that the mouthpiece is not contaminated with alcohol. |
| CONFIRM #: 950612092 OBSERVED (Y/N)? Y | Note the test number and then press the Enter key to continue. | Display shows the test number until the Enter key is pressed. The format is YYMMDDXXX where XXX is the test number. |
| CHECKING SUSTEM | Information only. No data entry required. | The isntrument is performing self-diagnostic checks. |
| PURGING | Information only. No data entry required. | Instrument is pruging the breath path with ambient air. |

| DISPLAY | KEYBOARD ENTRY | EXPLANATION |
|---|---|---|
| BLANK CHECK | Information only. No data entry required. | The instrument will flush the breath path with room air for approximately 30 seconds. A sample of this air is analyzed. If the result is .000, the Standard Check is initiated. If the result is >.000 a second purge is done. If a third blank result is >.000 the test is aborted. |
| BLANK .000   15:03<br>OBSERVED (Y/N)? Y | After observing the display press the Enter key. | |
| BLOW UNTIL BEEP<br>*********<br>TIME LEFT: 13:15 | If the subject refuses to submit a breath sample press the R key. The test will be aborted and the printer will print all of the subject data followed by "TEST REFUSED." | Instruct the subject to take a deep breath and blow into the mouthpiece as steadily and as long as possible. Flow and volume will be indicated by the * characters. |
| EVALUATING SAMPLE<br>RESULT 0.044 15:04 | Information only. No data entry required. | The Intox EC/IR evaluates the sample then prints the test results as shown below:<br>Confirmaion Test<br>Intox EC/IR<br>S/N: 01780<br>Location:<br>TEST SITE A49<br>Date: Mon 12 Jun 95<br>Time: 14:45<br>Test #: 950612092<br>Employee ID:<br>453 6125 23 |

|  |  | VALUE | TIME |
|---|---|---|---|
|  |  | (g/2101) |  |
|  | Blank | 0.000 | 15:02 |
|  | Result | 0.044 | 15:04 |

| DISPLAY | KEYBOARD ENTRY | EXPLANATION |
|---|---|---|
| PRINT ANOTHER COPY<br>(Y/N)? N | Press Y and the Enter key for another copy or press the Enter key to continue. | |
| RESULT 0.044 15:04<br>OBSERVED (Y/N)? Y | After observing the display press the Enter key. | |
| ATTACH PRINTOUT TO<br>FORM, PRESS ENTER | Attach the printout to the DOT alcohol test form then press Enter to continue. | |

| DISPLAY | KEYBOARD ENTRY | EXPLANATION |
|---------|----------------|-------------|
| COMPLETE FORM STEP 3 THEN PRESS ENTER | Complete Step 3 on the DOT test form and then press the Enter key to continue. | |
| COMPLETE FORM STEP 4 THEN PRESS ENTER | Complete Step 4 on the DOT test form and then press the Enter key to continue. | |
| PURGING | Information only. No data entry required. | Instrument is purging the breath path with ambient air. |

IF THE RESULT OF THE CONFIRMATION TEST IS GREATER THAN THE
"POSITIVE VALUE" SET UNDER F10-TANK SETUP, THEN THE DISPLAY WILL ASK
THE OPERATOR IF THEY WISH TO RUN AN ACCURACY CHECK. IF THE
OPERATOR RESPONDS YES, THEN AN AUTOMATIC ACCURACY CHECK WILL BE
INITIATED. THE STEPS DESCRIBING AN AUTOMATIC ACCURACY CHECK CAN BE
FOUND IN THE FOLLOWING SECTION UNDER F3-ACCURACY CHECK. IF THE
RESULT OF THE CONFIRMATION TEST IS LESS THAN THE "POSITIVE VALUE"
OR THE OPERATOR ANSWERS NO TO THE PROMPT FOR AN ACCURACY CHECK
THE INSTRUMENT WILL RETURN TO THE NORMAL SCROLLING MODE.

| | | |
|---------|----------------|-------------|
| Normal scrolling Mode | Information only. No data entry required. | The instrument returns to the Normal Scrolling Mode. |

## SUBJECT TESTS — ABORTS, REFUSALS AND ERRORS

### Aborting a Test

If you press the Esc key (Shift-Esc key for DOT protocol versions
or modes) at any point in this procedure, the instrument aborts
the test and indicates that the test has been aborted by the operator on the display and the printout.

### Time-outs and Refusals

The instrument waits for a predetermined period after the blow
message; "PLEASE BLOW," "BLOW UNTIL IT BEEPS" or
"BLOW UNTIL BEEP" appears. If the subject has not provided
a breath sample within that period, an appropriate message is
displayed and the printer prints a report showing that the test has
not been completed. The test number increments by one and the
display returns to scrolling mode. You may return to the Subject
Test by pressing the Return key and starting again. If you determine that the subject has refused to provide a sample while the

blow message is on the screen, press the "R" key and "TEST REFUSED" will be printed in the test result printout.

## Insufficient Breath Sample

If the subject does not provide a sufficient amount of breath, the instrument displays "INSUFFICIENT SAMPLE" and goes through another purging or testing cycle. After this cycle, the blow message appears again. At this point you may try another test after instructing the subject to take a deep breath and exhale completely.

If the subject cannot provide enough breath for a valid sample after the number of attempts allowed in the given protocol, the instrument aborts the process. "INSUFFICIENT SAMPLE" or "TEST REFUSED" shows on the display and the printer prints a report similar to the Subject Test report. The report does not show test results, but shows "INSUFFICIENT SAMPLE" or "TEST REFUSED" at the bottom.

## Recovery from Internal Printer Errors

If the printer is off line or the door latch has been left open at the end of the test, the display shows "CHECK PRINTER DOOR." Correct the problem by closing the door latch. If the printer is out of paper, "CHECK PRINTER PAPER" is displayed. Install a new roll of paper to correct this. In either case, after correcting the problem, set the printer on line by pressing the LINE/LOCAL push-button. The instrument will print the test results as soon as the problem is corrected and the printer is on line again.

# 7

# BLOOD AND URINE ANALYSIS

## §7.0    Blood Analysis

### §7.0.1    General Sources of Error

*Page 540.  Add at end of subsection:*

If a hospital conducts the blood analysis for alcohol, the enzymatic method of blood analysis may be employed. In such a case, counsel should be aware of a further possible source of error leading to falsely high BAC results: *ringer lactate.*

Dr. Robert Forrest of Sheffield University in England describes the phenomenon:

> Many hospitals use an enzymatic method to measure alcohol in blood. . . . The basis of the test is that the alcohol in the sample reacts with the enzyme alcohol dehydrogenase, present in the reagents used in the test, and is oxidised to acetaldehyde. In the process a linked reaction takes place and nicotinamide adenine nucleotide (NAD) is converted to NADH. The instrument actually measures the amount of alcohol present by following the increase in NADH which is proportional to the amount of alcohol present.
>
> If the enzyme lactate dehydrogenase is present in the sample and if high concentrations of lactate are present, then the lactate dehydrogenase will convert some of the lactate to pyruvate with the concomitant conversion of NAD to NADH. So if you have lactate and a high activity of lactate dehydrogenase present, then you will get a falsely elevated alcohol concentration.

You need both. If the enzymatic alcohol assay involves a stage where a protein precipant such as perchloric acid is added to the blood, which is then centrifuged, the clear supernatant fluid, which goes into the instruments does not contain any lactate dehydrogenase. Assays that do not include this step are vulnerable to false positive results.

High lactate dehydrogenase activities are found in some blood samples when the red blood cells have broken down or in patients with diseases as diverse as liver failure or pernicious anaemia.

So if you have ringer lactate infusion, plus an assay method for alcohol involving alcohol dehydrogenase which does not include a protein precipitation step, then you may well get a falsely elevated alcohol concentration in the sample. If it is measured by a gas chromatograph assay, however, there is no problem with ringer lactate.

To illustrate, last week I got a post mortem blood sample from another hospital. There was lots of lactate and lactate dehydrogenase in it. The other hospital got a result of 0.23 percent. I got a result of 0.00 percent with a gas chromatograph method.

# III

## PRE-TRIAL

# 10

---

# DISCOVERY

## §10.3    The Discovery Motion

### Page 701. Add at end of section:

The following is a second excellent version of a discovery motion, this one provided by noted DUI practitioner Douglas Cowan of Bellevue, Washington.* A "Notice of Non-Compliance and Motion to Compel" follows the discovery request, preparatory to a possible later demand for sanctions.

---

*Reprinted with permission.

## IN THE KING COUNTY DISTRICT COURT
## BELLEVUE DIVISION, STATE OF WASHINGTON

| | |
|---|---|
| STATE OF WASHINGTON, ) | |
| Plaintiff, ) | NO. 123456 |
| ) | |
| vs. ) | NOTICE OF APPEARANCE, |
| DEFENDANT, ) | DEMAND FOR JURY TRIAL, |
| Defendant. ) | DEMAND FOR DISCOVERY, |
| ) | BILL OF PARTICULARS, |
| ) | ASSERTION OF AFFIRMATIVE |
| ) | DEFENSE, AND OMNIBUS |
| ) | APPLICATION |
| ) | **CLERK'S ACTION REQUIRED** |

TO: Clerk of the Above-Entitled Court; and

TO: Prosecuting Attorney

**PLEASE TAKE NOTICE** that the below-named attorney hereby enters his appearance on behalf of the Defendant, DEFENDANT.

The defendant hereby enters a plea of Not Guilty and demands a jury trial, and demands discovery.

**FURTHER, PLEASE TAKE NOTICE** that, pursuant to the authority of CrR 4.7, CrRLJ 4.7, CrRLJ 6.13(c)(2), Local Rules governing dicovery, ER 705, RCW 10.58.010, 10.37.050, et seq., 46.61,502, 504 and 506, 42.17.260, the Fourth, Fifth, Sixth and Fourteenth Amendments to the United States Constitution, and art. 1, §§ 3, 7, 29, and 30, and the Tenth Amendment to the Washington State Constitution;

**THE DEFENDANT HEREBY** makes the following demands, motions, and requests for discovery in the matter(s) pending under this Cause Number:

### 1. Bill of Particulars

A written Bill of Particulars, including a description of all facts upon which the prosecution intends to rely to support the charge pending against the defendant, and a copy of the specific statute or ordinance under which the defendant is charged, along with a copy of any enabling legislation which adopts any other statute or ordinance by reference.

### 2. Assertion of Affirmative Defense

Defendant asserts that the Defendant consumed a sufficient quantity of alcohol after the time of driving and before the administration of any breath or blood test to cause Defendant's alcohol concentration to be .10 or more within two hours after driving; per *State v. Hornaday,* 105 Wash. 2d 120, 127 (1986).

### 3. Police Reports

Copies of any and all police or investigative reports (including field notes and/or blue book entries), and statements of all potential witnesses including *all* documentation of results of physical or mental examinations and/or scientific tests, experiments, or comparisons made in connection with the charge pending against the defendant;

### 4. List of Witnesses

The names and addresses of any and all persons whom the prosecution intends to call as witnesses at the hearing or trial, together with any and all written or recorded statements, and the substance of any oral statements of such witnesses, together with a summary of the expected testimony of any witness the plaintiff intends to call if the substance of the expected testimony is not contained in the materials otherwise provided;

### 5. Miranda Rights/242 Rights

Copies of any and all forms read to or signed by the defendant containing information regarding his rights under CrRLJ 3.1 and/or RCW 46.61.506 and 46.20.308, including information regarding the claimed basis for the arrest of the defendant and allegedly giving rise to the mandatory provisions of RCW 46.20,308;

### 6. Statements of Defendant/Demand for CrRLJ 3.5 Hearing

Copies of any written or recorded statements and the substance of any oral statements made by the Defendant. **Take notice that the Defendant hereby demands a hearing pursuant to CrRLJ 3.5** if the prosecution intends to offer any such statements at the time of trial;

### 7. Exhibits

A list of, copies of, and access to any books, papers, documents, photographs, diagrams, illustrative exhibits, or other tangible objects which the prosecution or any of its witnesses intend to use or make reference to at hearing or trial;

### 8. Items Seized from Defendant

A list of everything which was seized from or belonging to the defendant, regardless of whether the prosecution intends to introduce said items at hearing or trial;

### 9. Tape or Video Recordings, Etc.

Copies of or access to any recordings, video-tapes or tape recordings made of the defendant pursuant to the arrest of this case;

### 10. Prior Convictions

Any record of prior criminal conviction known to the prosecution of the defendant or persons whom the Prosecuting Attorney intends to call as witnesses at the hearing or trial;

### 11. Exculpatory Evidence

Disclosure of any material or information within the prosecution's knowledge which tends to negate the defendant's guilt as to the offense charged, or to any material element thereof;

### 12. 911 Tapes, Etc.

A copy of any "911 tapes" or other tape recordings containing information relative to this case and all radio broadcasts and tranmissions occurring between the officer(s) who detained, arrested and/or transported the defendant on the date of the alleged incident herein, and any other agency, officer, communications center or station during the course of the detention, arrest, transportation, testing and booking or charging defendant;

### 13. Radio Logs

A copy of all radio calls logged at the location of the breath test administered to the defendant ten minutes before through ten minutes after the time of the administration of the breath test concerned therein.

### 14. Photograph of DataMaster Test Machine

Timely inspection of and an opportunity to photograph the breath test machine used to test a sample of the defendant's breath herein;

### 15. Laboratory Procedures

A statement describing the "standard laboratory procedures" used to prepare the simulator solution as set forth in WAC 448-13-070, together with a copy of any protocol currently approved by the State Toxicologist for the preparation of simulator solutions as also described therein;

### 16. Software

A list of those versions of software currently approved for use in the BAC Verifier DataMaster as described in WAC 448-13-080;

### 17. Quality Assurance Program

A copy of the results of all tests performed pursuant to the quality assurance program described in WAC 448-13-100, together with copies of all protocols currently approved by the State Toxicologist for performing such tests;

### 18. Protocols

Copies of any protocols currently approved by the State Toxicologist for use in the administration of the breath test program as decribed in WAC 448-13-120.

### 19. DataMaster Records

A copy of the most current record of all breath tests administered on the particular machine along with the machine's evaluation, maintenance and certification records, including repairs, replacement of parts, unscheduled maintenance and reports of any malfunctions or difficulties by any person whomsoever in the history of the instrument's use, along with all documentary information relative to the machine's performance, including all records of complaints or observed problems with the machine which were reported by telephone or radio.

### 20. Blood/Breath Correlation Studies

Copies of all blood/breath correlation studies performed by the Washington State Patrol or other police agency whether formally conducted, or generated as a result of "informal drinking lab sessions";

### 21. Simulator Solution Test Results

A copy of the results of all gas chromatograph printouts of test performed on the simulator solution actually used in the test of the defendant's breath before and after the date of the test administered in this case.

### 22. Radio Frequency Interference

Any information regarding the presence of radios, microwaves, short waves, CBs and any other devices which emit radio frequency at or near the location of the breath testing instrument at or about the time of the administration of the test concerned herein, together with any and all information, test results, studies, memoranda, or other material from the manufacturer or any other source concerning the effects of "radio frequency interference" along with copies of all RFI tests performed on the machine in question known to the prosecution's expert witnesses or the Washington State Patrol crime lab personnel;

### 23. Interferant Studies

Copies of all experiments, studies, drinking labs, memos or other documentation of "interferants" on the DataMaster test results.

### 24. Mouth Alcohol Detection

Copies of all experiments, studies, drinking labs, memos or other documentation of the DataMaster's ability to detect mouth alcohol.

### 25. Preservation of Samples

Preservation of and access to any blood, breath, or urine samples taken from the defendant as a result of investigation of the charges pending herein for the purpose of re-testing the same;

### 26. Manuals

Copies of or access to the BAC Verifier DataMaster Training Manual, technical manuals, operator manuals, troubleshooting guides and maintenance manuals or bulletins and any other written materials utilized by the Washington State Patrol, State Toxicology Lab, or other law enforcement entity relating to the administration of blood or breath alcohol tests, or any written materials, including routine correspondence received by the Washington State Patrol from the current vendor of the BAC Verifier DataMaster or any supplier therefore;

### 27. Technician Blue Books

Copies of the "blue books" all DataMaster technicians who have worked on or maintained the machine in question over the past twelve months.

### 28. Mathematical Formulas

A copy of any mathematical formulas utilized in the BAC Verifier DataMaster in determining: (1) the acetone or other interferant measurement in a breath sample; (2) the alcohol content in a breath sample, or (3) any other mathematical formula or computation utilized in the BAC Verifier DataMaster at any stage of the process involved in the administration of a breath test;

### 29. Troubleshooting Guide

A copy of all current Troubleshooting Guides utilized by DataMaster technicians or electronic repair persons in the repair or maintenance of DataMaster machines.

### 30. Components in DataMaster

A list of the types and versions of the components approved for use in the relevant DataMaster machine as well as a list of those components *actually* used in the BAC Verifier DataMaster to test a sample of the defendant's breath herein, including but not limited to: Detector Board type and version; CPU Board type and version; Power Supply Board type and version; Breath Block type and version and Radio Frequency Interference Board type and version along with a copy of the document authorizing or approving the use of the component if it is different than that originally approved by the State Toxicologist.

### 31. Retrograde Extrapolation

The defendant demands notice if the prosecution intends to offer testimony regarding "retrograde extrapolation" and, if so, the name of the expert witnesss, his/her credentials, education, training and experience relevant thereto and disclosure of any documents, studies, reports or other materials relied on or material to any aspect of his or her testimony;

### 32. Widmark's Formula

The defendant demands notice if the prosecution intends to offer testimony regarding "Widmark's Formula" and, if so, the name of the expert witness, his/her credentials, education, training and experience and disclosure of any documents, studies, reports or other materials relied on or material to any aspect of his or her testimony;

### 33. Alcohol Impairment Testimony

The defendant demands notice if the prosecution intends to offer medical or scientific testimony regarding the effects of alcohol on driving ability, physical or mental impairment, etc., and, if so, the name of the expert witness, his/her credentials, education, training and experience and disclosure of any documents, studies, reports or other materials relied on or material to any aspect of his or her testimony;

### 34. Operator's Qualifications

A copy of the permit issued by the State Toxicologist to the **operator** who administered any test of the defendant's breath or blood, the effective dates of that permit, together with a description of the training taken by that operator which qualified him/her for certification, along with the dates and places that training was completed;

### 35. Instructor's Qualifications

A copy of the permit issued by the State Toxicologist to the instructor who trained the operator referred to in paragraph 32, above, together with a description of the training taken by that instructor which qualified him/her for certification, along with the dates and places that training was completed;

### 36. Technician's Qualifications

A copy of the permit issued by the State Toxicologist to any **technician** who performed maintenance, repair, adjustment, regular service, or any other work whatsoever on the DataMaster used in the administration of the breath test to the Defendant herein, together with a description of the training taken by that instructor which qualified him/her for certification, along with the dates and places that training was completed;

### 37. Solution Changer's Qualifications

A copy of the permit issued by the State Toxicologist to the individual **who most recently changed the simulator solution** prior to the date on which the Defendant herein submitted to a test of his/her breath on the BAC Verifier DataMaster used herein, together with a description of the training taken by that solution changer which qualified him/her for certification, along with the dates and places that training was completed;

### 38. Radar Demand

If the prosecution intends to offer radar evidence on any issue raised herein at motions or trial, the defense demands, pursuant to CrRLJ 6.13 and other applicable rules, the production of an electronic speed measuring device (SMD) expert at motions or trial, and objects to the introduction at motions or trial of any certificate or affidavit concerning the design, operation or construction of any such speed measuring device.

### 39. Experts Demanded at Trial

The defendant objects to proof of any material fact at hearing or trial by affidavit or certificate. A certified BAC Verifier DataMaster technician *and* the person(s) who conducted any quality assurance tests as well as the person(s) responsible for preparing, storing and installing the simulator solution concerned herein **IS HEREBY DEMANDED AT HEARING OR TRIAL,** including any and all records pertaining to the preparation, checking and installation of the simulator solution used in this case, including the gas chromatograph charts regarding the solution in accordance with CrRLJ 6.13 and RCW 46.61.506(6), along with a copy of his or her permit.

**IF THE PROSECUTOR INTENDS TO OFFER SAID WITNESSES AS "EXPERT WITNESSES"**, Defendant requests discovery of his or her education and training, both general and specific to the subject of his or her testimony, experience relative to the operation, maintenance, and theory of the instrument used to test the defendant's blood or breath, or simulator solution and a description of the place, date, and subject matter of all training taken by said witnesses have participated or about which he or she may testify, and any documents, studies, reports or other materials relied on or material to any aspect of his or her testimony;

### 40. Any Other Experts Demanded

The disclosure and presence of any other expert witnesses **IS HEREBY DEMANDED AT HEARING OR TRIAL** along with a copy of his or her qualifications, together with all information requested in paragraph 32, above, regarding the subject matter of said witnesses testimony.

### 41. Speedy Trial Demanded

Defendant objects to the date of arraignment, demands trial within the time period required by CrRLJ 3.3, objects to any trial date not so set and moves the court for an order setting a trial date within the speedy trial rule time limits;

### 42. Objection to Citation/Complaint

Defendant further objects to the sufficiency of the charging document, the failure of the prosecution to properly verify it, objects to the untimely filing of same and moves to dismiss all charges pending herein;

43. **Failure to Comply**

**YOU ARE FURTHER NOTIFIED** that failure to comply with these requests will result in the defendant moving for appropriate relief at time of hearing or trial.

Dated this 11th day of June, 1999.

_____
DOUGLAS COWAN
Attorney for Defendant
WSBA# 2146

## IN THE KING COUNTY DISTRICT COURT
## BELLEVUE DIVISION, STATE OF WASHINGTON

STATE OF WASHINGTON, )
     Plaintiff,       )   NO. 123456
                      )
     vs.             )
DEFENDANT,        )   NOTICE OF NON-
     Defendant.     )   COMPLIANCE, SECOND
                      )   DEMAND FOR DISCOVERY &
                      )   MOTION TO COMPEL

**COMES NOW** the Defendant by and through her attorney of record, Douglas L. Cowan, and hereby notifies the prosecuting attorney in the above-referenced case that the materials provided in response to Defendant's original Demand for Discovery are incomplete and non-responsive to the requests made therein and do not comply with the requirements of CrR4.7, CrRLJ 4.7, CrRLJ 6.13(c)(2), applicable Local Court Rules governing discovery, RCW 46.61.506 and the due process provisions of the Washington State Constitutions, to-wit: The prosecution has failed to respond to the discovery demand regarding information on retrograde extrapolation and Widmark's formula, and the name of the specific breath technician to be called in this case, together with the information demanded regarding said witness in Defendant's original Demand for Discovery.

The defendant hereby makes this Second Demand for Discovery and moves the Court for an Order compelling compliance in order to allow adequate time to prepare for the trial of the matters pending herein.

**PLEASE TAKE NOTICE** that failure to comply with the required information by _____, one week before trial, will result in a motion to suppress the results of the breath test herein.

**DATED:** _____

_____
DOUGLAS COWAN
Attorney for Defendant
WSBA# 2146

# 11

## SUPPRESSION OF EVIDENCE

### §11.1    Sobriety Checkpoints: Sitz

*Page 728.   Add after numbered list:*

Since the *Sitz* decision, the Supreme Court has come to a seemingly contradictory result in a case involving *drug* roadblocks. In
*City of Indianapolis v. Edmond* (No. 99-1030; Nov. 28, 2000),__
U.S.__, the Court in a 6-3 decision found a violation of the Fourth
Amendment when police stopped cars at a checkpoint, looked
into them, examined the drivers' licenses/registration, and led
drug-sniffing dogs around them. The distinction from *Sitz*, the
majority explained, was that the "primary purpose" of the drug
roadblock was "to uncover evidence of ordinary criminal wrongdoing" — as opposed to the sobriety checkpoint that's purpose is
to "protect public safety." Query the logic of that distinction. Interestingly, Justice Thomas in his dissent wrote, "I am not con-
vinced that *Sitz* and *Martinez-Fuentes* were correctly decided.
Indeed, I rather doubt that the Framers of the Fourth Amendment would have considered 'reasonable' a program of indiscrim-
inate stops of individuals not suspected of wrongdoing."

### §11.1.1    Evasion of Sobriety Checkpoints

*Page 735.   Add at end of carryover paragraph:*

See also *Ingersoll v. Palmer*, 43 Cal. 3d 1321, 1336 (1987); *U.S. v.
Ogilvie*, 527 F.2d 330 (9th Cir. 1975).

*Page 735. Add at end of subsection:*

More recently, the U.S. Court of Appeals for the Ninth Circuit, dealing with a California border patrol checkpoint case, has similarly responded in the negative. In *U.S. v. Montero-Camargo*, 208 F.3d 1123 (9th Cir. April 11, 2000, #97-50643), border patrol agents were tipped that two cars with Mexicali license plates had turned around south of a checkpoint at El Centro. The drivers were stopped and taken back to the checkpoint, where searches of the cars produced two bags of marijuana. The defendant's motion to suppress on the grounds that there was no reasonable suspicion of criminal activity to justify the initial stop was denied.

The Ninth Circuit Court began by noting the general rule that "avoidance of a checkpoint, without more, is insufficient to support a finding of reasonable suspicion," citing *U.S. v. Ogilvie (supra)*. The court then went on, however, to find that there were additional factors in the case before them that did support "reasonable suspicion": the cars had Mexican plates, the drivers were Hispanic, the area was a common one for drug deals and "turn-arounds." The dissenting opinion found these other factors dubious.

Clearly, then in the drunk driving case the officer must be able to point to something more than an apparent avoidance of the checkpoint, such as making an illegal U-turn.

## §11.5   Field Evidence

### §11.5.2   Field Sobriety Tests

*Page 773. Add at end of subsection:*

Law enforcement agencies across the country have begun using so-called standardized field sobriety tests (FSTs). These consist of a battery of three tests (walk-and-turn, one-leg stand, and nystagmus), which must be given exactly as set forth by the National Highway Traffic Safety Administration (NHTSA); the tests are objectively scored. All other tests previously used by various agencies have been found to be ineffective.

Prosecutors and law enforcement agencies in some states have resisted this clear trend. While actually copying NHTSA's techniques for the three tests in many of their own manuals, officers pretend to be ignorant of any standardized method of testing — thus permitting continued subjective scoring and the use of such discredited tests as finger-to-nose, "modified position of attention," alphabet recitation, etc. Many law enforcement and prosecution agencies prefer the absence of any standards in drunk driving investigations. The only legal grounds for the continued admissibility of non-standardized tests (including standardized tests performed in a non-standardized manner), however, appears to be "We've always done it that way!"

That situation must change, as it is changing in other states. In *State v. Homan*, 732 N.E.2d 952 (Ohio 2000), for example, the Ohio Supreme Court has ruled that "(i)n order for the results of a field sobriety test to serve as evidence of probable cause to arrest, the police must have administered the test in strict accordance with standardized testing procedures." In that case, the state trooper actually gave the three NHTSA standardized FSTs that are now required in that state — but he failed to administer them in strict accordance with the standards, resulting in suppression of all tests. The court noted with approval NHTSA's conclusion that "field sobriety tests are an effective means of detecting legal intoxication 'only when: the tests are administered in the prescribed, standardized manner, the standardized clues are used to assess the suspect's performance, (and) the standardized criteria are employed to interpret that performance.'"

Specifically, the court found the following flaws in the trooper's administration of the FSTs — flaws which would be considered common among most law enforcement officers:

> During cross-examination, Trooper Worcester testified that, in administering to appellee the HGN and walk-and-turn tests, he at times deviated from established testing procedures. With respect to the HGN test, for example, Trooper Worcester testified that, in observing appellee's eyes for nystagmus at maximum deviation, he did not hold appellee's eyes at maximum deviation for a full four seconds as standardized procedures require. In addition, in determining at what angle appellee's eyes began to exhibit nystagmus, Trooper Worcester did not, as recommended, move the stimulus at a pace that would take a full four seconds to move appellee's

eyes from a forward gaze to the right. It took Trooper Worcester only one to two seconds to make the pass.

Trooper Worcester also admitted to deviating from established police practice by conducting the walk-and-turn test between his patrol car and appellee's car. In addition, Trooper Worcester gave appellee the option of turning either to the right or the left after completing the required number of steps. Police procedure requires that the suspect turn to the left. . . .The record also indicates that the walk-and-turn test was conducted on a gravel covered, uneven surface of road when a flat surface is required to perform the test.

It should be apparent that as the NHTSA standardized tests become widely accepted — and non-standardized tests fall from use — a new *Kelly-Daubert* standard for admissibility is being created for field sobriety tests. The old tests are no longer "widely accepted" as a valid means of detecting impairment or intoxication, and the old methods of administering approved tests are no longer up to the professional standard. It remains only for attorneys to begin challenging the admissibility of the tests in court.

The following material will give the reader a firm understanding of the theory and development of the standardized field sobriety tests in arguing for suppression. (For a more detailed discussion of the administration of the tests themselves, see §4.3.) The author is grateful to George L. Bianchi of Seattle, Washington, for his kind permission to reproduce this edited version of his excellent work.

---

In June of 1975, the Southern California Research Institute was commissioned by NHTSA to study and evaluate the then currently used "field sobriety tests" to determine their alcohol sensitivity, develop more sensitive and reliable tests, and attempt to standardize the administration of "field sobriety tests." In this regard, they were looking to physical coordination tests associated with a DUI investigation to determine, if possible, their relationship to intoxication and posssibly driving impairment. The goal was to develop alcohol-sensitive tests that would provide more reliable evidence by standardizing the tests themselves and the observations to be made. The end result was *Psycho-Physical Tests for DWI Arrests,* DOTHS 802 424, (Burns & Moskowitz, June 1977). Some of the original sixteen "tests" considered were AGN, walk-and-turn, Romberg-balance, finger-to-nose, one-leg-stand, and finger-count or finger-dexterity. Reciting the alphabet and counting backwards were not ever considered. To make the tests more reliable and objective (as opposed to subjective), the authors pursued the development of a "test battery" which would provide statistically valid and reliable indications that a driver's breath alcohol concentration (BrAC) level was at or above 0.10, rather than indications of driver impairments. *Validation of the Standardized Field Sobriety Test Battery at BAC's Below 0.10 Percent,* DOTHS _____ at page 28, (Stuster & Burns, August 1998). Certain tests were originally eliminated because they were determined to not be alcohol sensitive. The result was a pilot program that studied a six-test battery (one-leg-stand, walk-and-run, finger-to-nose, finger-count, Gaze Nystagmus and tracing) with three alternates (Romberg-balance, subtraction, counting backwards and letter cancellation). The original data in the 1977 study suggested that it was unrealistic to attempt to use behavioral tests to discriminate BrAC's in a plus or minus 0.02 margin around the given BrAC level of 0.10 percent. *Psycho-Physical Tests for DWI Arrests,* at page 41. The authors also noted an obvious unacceptable error rate of 47 percent in "arresting" individuals who were under a BrAC of 0.10 percent. *Id.* at page 28, 30 and Appendix 6, page 102. Some of the sources of error were determined to be the failure of officers to heed the lack of test evidence, impairment which was *not* alcohol related and officers who did *not* score the tests properly. *Id.* at page 28. The study resulted in a three-test battery that included alcohol Gaze Nystagmus, the one-leg-stand and walk-and-turn test. The authors stated

> It became apparent during field visits that this objective [standardization of the tests and observation procedures] is highly important. There are wide differences between officers in using tests to assess a driver's state of intoxication, and they may exist within the department as well as between agencies and locales. These differences seriously detract from reliability as well as from credibility of the officers in court proceedings.

*Id.* at page 59.

　　The standardization of the three-test battery occurred in 1981 with *Development and Field Tests of Psycho-Physical Tests for DWI Arrests,*

DOTHS 805 864, (Tharp, Burns & Moskowitz, March 1981). The authors defined a standardized test as:

> One which the procedures, apparatus and scoring have been fixed so that precisely the same testing procedures can be followed at different times and locations.

*Id.* at page 3.

From August of 1978 untill March of 1981 when the final report was concluded, Tharp, Burns and Moskowitz worked to standardize the administration and scoring procedures associated with the three-test battery (walk-and-turn test, the one-leg-stand test and Horizontal Gaze Nystagmus). Their results were evaluated in the laboratory and to a *limited* extent, in the field. *Development and Field Tests for DWI Arrests,* DOTHS 805 864 (Tharp, Burns & Moskowitz, March 1981).

As it relates to the walk-and-turn test, the authors noted that requesting people to "watch their feet" while performing this test increased its sensitivity to alcohol, but made the test difficult for people with monocular vision (i.e., poor depth perception). Performing the walk-and-turn test with the eyes open and enough light to see some frame of reference was determined to be essential if sober individuals were to perform the test without difficulty. *Id.* at page 4. Certain individuals were noted to have difficulty with the walk-and-turn test when sober, including people over 65 years of age, people with back, leg or middle ear problems, and people with high-heeled shoes (over 2 inches). *Id.* at page 5. The authors determined that the test required a line which the police officer could manufacture. They also recommended that the walk-and-turn test be performed on a dry, hard, level, non-slippery surface and under relatively safe conditions. If those requirements could not be met at the roadside, that the suspect be asked to perform the test elsewhere or that only the Nystagmus test be used. *Id.* at page 5.

As it relates to the one-leg-stand test, the authors ascertained that the suspect must be able to see in order to orient himself or herself and the police officer must stand back from the suspect in order not to provide an artificial reference frame which could distract the suspect. Generally, if the suspect could not see or orient with respect to a perpendicular frame of reference, then the test was determiend to be difficult even if sober. *Id.* at page 5. Again, the authors noted that certain individuals would have difficulty performing the one-leg-stand test under sober conditions, including people over the age of 65, people with leg, back or middle ear problems, and people who are overweight by 50 or more pounds. Lastly, the authors recommended that the one-leg-stand test be performed only on a hard, dry, level, non-slippery surface and under relatively safe conditions and if those requirements could not be met at the roadside, that the suspect be asked to perform the test elsewhere or that only the Nystagmus test be used. *Id.* at page 5.

As it relates to the Gaze Nystagmus, the author noted that approximately half of the "sober" people tested showed a slight Nystagmus in at least one eye when their eyes were deviated maximally. *Id.* at page 7. The authors recommended that corrective lenses should be removed prior to the administration of this test. *Id.* at page 7. They also recommended that in looking for the onset of Nystagmus, the stimulus be moved fairly slowly (i.e., at about 10 degrees per second), otherwise normal oscillation of the eyeball may be mistaken for Nystagmus. *Id.* at page 7. On the second movement of the stimulus in each direction, the recommendation was that the stimulus be moved faster (about 20 degrees per second) and that the observer should note whether or not the suspect can follow smoothly and how distinct the Nystagmus is at the maximum lateral deviation. *Id.* at page 9. The authors conclued that the Gaze Nystagmus test may not be applicable to individuals wearing contact lenses, since hard contacts prevent extreme lateral eye movements. *Id.* at page 9. Also of note is that the authors indicated that Gaze Nystagmus could be seen in 50 to 60 percent of all individuals if their eyes were deviated to the extremes and that Gaze Nystagmus occurs with some types of brain damage. *Id.* at page 92.

In discussing alcohol and balance, the authors noted that other variables, in addition to alcohol, could increase body sway, such as sleep loss, increasing of room temperature and eating. *Id.* at 83. They also concluded that one of the most important parameters in tests of balance and muscular coordination is vision. In their opinion, closing the eyes makes all of the balance tests much more difficult for sober and intoxicated individuals. *Id.* at 83. The data, to them, suggested that peripheral vision plays a particularly important role in maintaining balance. *Id.* at 84.

The end result of the 1981 study was an indication that the Gaze Nystagmus could correctly classify individuals at or above a BrAC of 0.10 seventy-seven percent (77%) of the time, that the walk-and-turn test could properly classify individuals as being at or above a BrAC of 0.10 sixty-eight percent (68%) of the time and the one-leg-stand test could properly classify individuals at or above a BrAC of 0.10 sixty-five percent (65%) of the time. When they combined the results of the Gaze Nystagmus with the walk-and-turn test, there was determined to be an 80 percent accurate classification of a person at or above a BrAC of 0.10 level. The authors also noticed a 32 percent false arrest rate in the overall statistics.

In 1983 the NHTSA commissioned Anderson, Schweitz and Snyder to develop standardized practical and effective procedures for police officers to use in reaching an arrest/no arrest decision. *Field Evaluation of Behavioral Test Battery for DWI,* DOTHS 806 475 (Anderson, Schweitz & Snyder, September 1983). The study tested the feasibility of using the three-test battery in the operational conditions by police officers and was to secure data to help determine if the three-test battery would discriminate as well in the field as it had previously in the laboratory. The end results of this study mirrored the statistical results of the laboratory testing previously summarized in 1981 by Tharp, Burns and Moskowitz in *Development and Field Tests for DWI Arrest.*

Jack Stuster and Marcelline Burns were commissioned by the National Highway Traffic Safety Institute to evaluate the accuracy of the standardized field sobriety test battery to assist officers in making arrest decisions for DWI at alcohol concentrations below 0.10 percent. In August of 1998, Their report was submitted to the National Highway Traffic Safety Administration. *Validation of the Standardized Field Sobriety Test Battery at BAC's Below 0.10 Percent,* DOTHS _____ (Stuster & Burns, August 1998). As the authors noted:

> During the past sixteen years, NHTSA's SFSTs largely have repaced the invalidated performance tests of unknown merit that once were the patrol officers only in helping to make post-stop DWI arrest decisions. Regional and local preferences for other performance tests still exists, even though some of the tests have never been validated. Despite regional differences and what tests are used to assist officers in making DWI arrest decisions, NHTSA's SFSTs pres-

ently are used in all 50 states. NHTSA's SFSTs have become the standard pre-arrest procedures for evaluating DWI in most law enforcement agencies.

*Id.* at 3. The authors also found that prosecutors who were interviewed suggested that the optimum situation would be for all law enforcement agencies to restrict their field sobriety evaluations to the same standardized battery of three tests. *Id.* at 24. The 1998 study showed that the Gaze Nystagmus test had the highest correlation of accuracy when compared to the actual measured breath test level. In this regard the Gaze Nystagmus test showed a 65 percent correlation to the actual measured alcohol level. The walk-and-turn test resulted in a 61 percent correlation to the actual measured alcohol concentration level, with the one-leg-stand test showing a 45 percent correlation with the actual measured alcohol level. *Id.* at 17. Approximately 10 percent of the individuals were determined to be falsely arrested by law enforcement in that their alcohol level was estimated to have been greater than 0.08 percent, but later found to be below that level. *Id.* at 18. Of interest is the range of BrAC that is *not* measured and correlated in the 297 individuals tested. The range of BrAC tested is from a .038 for 8 underage females to a 0.07 for 2 underage females. There were no individuals whose measured BrAC level reflected 0.08 up to approximately 0.13 percent in the study. Thus, no individuals were tested at BrAC levels ranging from what appears to be a 0.08 up to and including a 0.13 which resulted in the above-listed statistical analysis. *Id.* at 16.

As a result of the above studies, the National Highway Traffic Safety Administration published both student and instructor manuals to be used by law enforcement agencies for the detection and arrest of DWI suspects. *DWI Detection and Standardized Field Sobriety Testing.* The first set of manuals were printed in 1981 with subsequent publications in 1992 (PB 94-780228 Student Manual, PB 94-780210 Instructor Manual), 1995 (AVA-19911BB00 Student Manual, AVA-19910BB00 Instructor Manual) and 2000 (AVA 20839-BB0 Student Manual, AVA 20838-BB0 Instructor Manual). These manuals provided to law enforcement do *not* incorporate the statistical results of Stuster and Burns wherein they attempt to validate the three tests SFST battery to alcohol levels below 0.10 pecent. These manuals incorporate and instruct law enforcement on the statistical results of the three studies leading up to and including *Field Evaluation of Behavioral Test Battery for DWI,* DOTHS 806 475 (Anderson, Schweitz & Snyder, September 1983).

## SUMMARY OF NATIONAL HIGHWAY TRAFFIC SAFETY ADMINISTRATION STUDENT AND INSTRUCTOR MANUALS FOR DWI DETECTION AND STANDARDIZED FIELD SOBRIETY TESTING

The National Highway Traffic Safety Adminstration has defined DWI detection as:

> The entire process of identifying and gathering evidence to determine whether or not a suspect should be arrested for a DWI violation.

1995 SFST Student Manual (AVA-19911BB00) at page IV-1; 1995 SFST Instructor Manual (AVA-19910BB00) at page IV-1. DWI detection is divided into three phases. Phase one being the vehicle in motion, phase two being personal contact and phase three being pre-arrest screening. 1995 SFST Student Manual at IV-2-5, 1995 SFST Instructor Manual at IV-1-5.

Phase one involves observing the vehicle in motion and deciding whether there is sufficient cause to command the driver to stop. 1995 SFST Student Manual at IV-3-5, V-1-12, 1995 SFST Instructor Manual at IV-1-2, V-1-15.

Phase two is personal contact with an individual. At this time the officer is to observe and interview the driver, face to face, in order to decide whether there is sufficient cause to instruct the driver to step from the vehicle for further investigation. 1995 SFST Student Manual, IV-3-4, IV-1-14. It is at this point the officer makes observations to determine whether or not it is appropriate to order the individual to exit his vehicle to perform the standardized field sobriety testing.

Phase three is defined as "pre-arrest screening" to determine if there is probable cause to arrest the suspect for DWI by the use of the standardized field sobriety testing (psycho-physical tests) which have been identified and *validated* through NHTSA's research program. 1995 SFST Student Manual IV, Section VII & VIII. 1995 SFST Instructor Manual, Section VII & VIII.

Proper training of a law enforcement officer under the *NHTSA DUI DETECTION AND STANDARDIZED FIELD SOBRIETY*

*TESTING* curriculum consists of 16 sessions that span 22 hours, 45 minutes of instruction, *excluding* breaks. While NHTSA recognizes there may be some need of flexibility in the curriculum, they state that:

> It is the IACP (International Association of Chiefs of Police) and NHTSA's position that students cannot be assured of achieving proficiency in using and interpreting the standardized field sobriety testing if the sessions dealing with that topic are curtailed in scope or duration.

1995 SFST Instructor Manual at page 6.

> THE STANDARDIZED FIELD SOBRIETY TESTS ARE NOT AT ALL FLEXIBLE. THEY MUST BE ADMINISTERED EACH TIME, EXACTLY AS OUTLINED IN THIS COURSE.

1995 SFST Instructor Manual at page 10.

NHTSA emphasizes that the results of the three studies they commissioned validated the standardized field sobriety tests, yet emphasized one final and major point.

> THIS VALIDATION APPLIES *ONLY* WHEN THE TESTS ARE ADMINISTERED IN THE PRESCRIBED STANDARDIZED MANNER; AND *ONLY* WHEN THE STANDARDIZED CLUES ARE USED TO ASSESS THE SUSPECT'S PERFORMANCE; AND, *ONLY* WHEN THE STANDARDIZED CRITERIA ARE EMPLOYED TO INTERPRET THAT PERFORMANCE.
>
> IF ANY ONE OF THE STANDARDIZED FIELD SOBRIETY TEST ELEMENTS IS CHANGED, THE VALIDITY IS COMPROMISED.

1995 SFST Student Manual, VIII-12 (see also 1995 SFST Instructor Manual, VIII-8, where it is stated that "if any of the standardized elements of the test are changed, their validity will be threatened.")

## CONCLUSION

In the absence of foundation testimony establishing the reliability and relevance of field sobriety tests and physical observations to show alcohol-induced impairment of the ability to drive a motor vehicle, such test results and observations should be excluded from use as that type of evidence. In any trial which does not involve a breath test, it is evident from the above-discussed studies that the standardized field sobriety tests are not relevant and should not be admissible in the DUI trial.

Before such testimony should be introduced it must be shown to be relevant and more probative than prejudicial. In order to show this requisite probative value, a foundation must be laid showing that there is a physiological relationship between the consumption of alcohol and the decreased ability to perform the specific physical tests requested by the officer. In the absence of such showing, the prosecution should be precluded from making any reference to said tests. In the absence of a proper foundation, the tests are either irrelevant or unduly prejudicial. The court went on further to state that there must be *strict* compliance by the law enforcement officer with the NHTSA standards. (This is as opposed to substantial compliance.) In ruling the need for *strict* compliance, The Ohio Supreme Court stated:

> In the substantial-compliance cases, the minor procedural deviations that were at issue in no way affected the ultimate results. In contrast, it is well established that in field sobriety testing even minor deviations from the standardized procedures can severely bias the results. Moreover, our holdings in the substantial-compliance cases were grounded, at least in part, on the practical impossibility of strictly complying with the applicable adminstrative regulations. In contrast, we find that strict compliance with standardized field sobriety testing procedures is neither unrealistic nor humanly impossible in the great majority of vehicles stops in which the police choose to administer the tests.

*Homan* at page 426. Attached as Appendix C is the case of *State v. Homan.*

We, as attorneys, should demand that courts analyze "field sobriety tests," question their relevance and rule on their admissibility or use in light of the numerous scientific studies commissioned by the National Highway Traffic Safety Administration. Until the required foundational training and background of the arrestng officer is presented, the results of standardized field sobriety tests as well as any reference to them as "sobriety tests" must be suppressed.

## §11.6   Blood-Alcohol Evidence

### §11.6.7   The Physician-Patient Privilege (Blood)

*Page 825, change citation in fourth full paragraph:*

42 U.S.C. §290 (dd) (2).

### §11.6.12   Chain of Custody

*Page 852. Add new section after checklist:*

## §11.7   The Suppression Motion

The laws and pleading requirements concerning motions to suppress evidence vary widely from state to state. Usually, there will be a focus on one issue, such as the lack of probable cause to stop the client, and extensive argument and case law will be presented. The following sample motion, however, represents an "omnibus" approach applicable with some modification to most jurisdictions: a succinct yet comprehensive motion addressing a broad number of typical pretrial issues in a DUI case — addressing *both* suppression *and* discovery. The motion, authored by Douglas Cowan of Bellevue, Washington,* should keep any prosecutor busy for some time.

*Reprinted with permission.

## IN THE KING COUNTY DISTRICT COURT
## BELLEVUE DIVISION, STATE OF WASHINGTON

| | | |
|---|---|---|
| STATE OF WASHINGTON, | ) | |
| Plaintiff, | ) | NO. 123456 |
| | ) | |
| vs. | ) | |
| DEFENDANT, | ) | |
| Defendant. | ) | DEFENDANT'S PRETRIAL |
| | ) | MOTIONS AND ORDERS |
| | ) | THEREON |
| | ) | **NOTE FOR MOTION HEARING** |

**COMES NOW** the Defendant, DEFENDANT, by and through his attorney, and hereby files for hearing the following motions:

## I. SUPPRESSION/DISMISSAL.

### 1. Mandatory Filing

To dismiss based on the failure to comply with mandatory filing requirements of CrRLJ 2.1(d)(1) and (2), *State v. Greenwood,* 120 Wash. 2d 585 (1993) and *Seattle v. Bonifacio,* 127 Wash. 2d 482 (1995).

Motion is:  granted  _____
denied  _____
reserved  _____

### 2. Portable Breath Test

To suppress any breath test results performed on a portable breath test machine. *Frye v. United States,* 293 F.2d 1013 (D.C. Cir. 1923); *Seattle v. Peterson,* 39 Wash. App. 524 (1985); *State v. Cauthron,* 120 Wash. 2d 879 (1993); *State v. Riker,* 123 Wash. 2d 351 (1994); *Bokor v. Department of Licensing,* 74 Wash. App. 523 (1994); RCW 46.61.506(3).

Motion is:  granted  _____
denied  _____
reserved  _____

### 3. Gaze Nystagmus

To suppress the results of any nystagmus "gaze test" administered to the Defendant in this matter. *Frye v. United States,* 293

F.2d 1013 (D.C. Cir. 1923); *Seattle v. Peterson,* 39 Wash. App. 524 (1985); *State v. Cissne,* 72 Wash. App. 677 (1994); RCW 46.61.605(3).

Motion is:  granted  _____
denied  _____
reserved  _____

### 4. Speed Measuring Device

To suppress all evidence gathered following the use of any speed measuring device (SMD) and/or as a basis for the stop of the defendant. *Frye v. United States,* 293 F.2d 1013 (D.C. Cir. 1923); *Seattle v. Peterson,* 39 Wash. App. 524 (1985); *State v. Cauthron,* 120 Wash. 2d. 879 (1993); *State v. Riker,* 123 Wash. 2d 351 (1994); CrRLJ 6.13(d).

Motion is:  granted  _____
denied  _____
reserved  _____

### 5. SMD Certificates

For production of an electronic speed measuring device (SMD) expert at motions and trial herein and objects to the admission of any certificate or affidavit in lieu of live testimony concerning the design, operation or construction of any such speed measuring device at motions hearing or trial. CrRLJ 6.13.

Motion is:  granted  _____
denied  _____
reserved  _____

### 6. Pupil Dilation

To suppress any testimony regarding pupil dilation and/or reaction to light observations. *Frye v. United States,* 293 F.2d 1013 (D.C. Cir. 1923); *Seattle v. Peterson,* 39 Wash. App. 524 (1985); *State v. Cauthron,* 120 Wash. 2d. 879 (1993); *State v. Riker,* 123 Wash. 2d 351 (1994).

Motion is:  granted  _____
denied  _____
reserved  _____

### 7. Probable Cause

To suppress evidence based on a violation of RCW 46.64.015, RCW 46.61.021 and Art. 1, § 7 of the Washington State Constitution in that there was a lack of probable cause to stop, detain, or arrest the defendant herein. *Terry v. Ohio,* 392 U.S. 1 (1968); *State v. Thornton,* 41 Wash. App. 506 (1985); *State v. Michaels,* 60 Wash. 2d 638 (1962); CrRLJ 3.6.

Motion is:   granted   _____
                       denied    _____
                       reserved  _____

### 8. Consent to FSTs

To suppress physical tests for failure to obtain a valid consent from the defendant prior to the administration of said tests. *Seattle v. Personeus,* 63 Wash. App. 461 (1991); *Seattle v. Mesiani,* 110 Wash. 2d 454 (1988).

Motion is:   granted   _____
                       denied    _____
                       reserved  _____

### 9. Admissibility of FSTs

To suppress all evidence obtained in the course of "field sobriety" or other physical agility tests administered to the Defendant herein. Washington Const. Art. 1, § 7; U.S. Const. Amend. IV, *Frye v. United States,* 293 F.2d 1013 (D.C. Cir. 1923); *Seattle v. Peterson,* 39 Wash. App. 524 (1985); *State v. Cauthron,* 120 Wash. 2d. 879 (1993); *State v. Riker,* 123 Wash. 2d. 351 (1994).

Motion is:   granted   _____
                       denied    _____
                       reserved  _____

### 10. Testimonial FSTs

To suppress those physical tests which were testimonial in nature, not preceded by Miranda Warnings. CrRLJ 3.5 and *Pennsylvania v. Muniz,* 110 S. Ct. 2638, 110 L. Ed. 2d 528 (1990).

Motion is:   granted   _____
                       denied    _____
                       reserved  _____

### 11. Corpus Delicti

To dismiss the charge on the grounds that the prosecution is unable to prove the required element of identification of the defendant as the driver, in that there is insufficient evidence of the *corpus delicti* of the crime independent of the defendant's statements, pursuant to *State v. Hamrick,* 19 Wash. App. 417 (1978), et. al.; *Bremerton v. Corbett,* 106 Wash. 2d 569 (1986).

Motion is:   granted   _____
                       denied    _____
                       reserved  _____

## 12. Defendant's Statements

To suppress all statements attributed to the defendant at the time of arrest. *Edwards v. Arizona*, 451 U.S. 477 (1981); *State v. Johnson*, 48 Wash. App. 681 (1987), and for a pretrial hearing pursuant to CrRLJ 3.5.

Motion is:  granted  _____

denied  _____

reserved  _____

## 13. Right to Counsel

To dismiss or, in the alternative, suppress evidence due to violation of the right to counsel based on Wash. Const. Art. 1, § 22; U.S. Const. Amend. VI; *State v. Fitzsimmons*, 93 Wash. 2d 436 (1980); *Arizona v. Holland*, 711 P.2d 592 (1985); and *Spokane v. Kruger*, 116 Wash. 2d 135 (1991); *State v. Prok*, 107 Wash. 2d 153 (1986); *Seattle v. Box*, 29 Wash. App. 109 (1981); *Seattle v. Koch*, 53 Wash. App. 352 (1991), *State v. Easter*, 130 Wash. 2d 228 (1996).

Motion is:  granted  _____

denied  _____

reserved  _____

## 14. Refusal

To suppress any alleged refusal to perform any test pursuant to ER 403 and *State v. Long*, 113 Wash. 2d. 266, (1989); *State v. Parker*, 16 Wash. App. 632 (1976); *Seattle v. Personeus*, 63 Wash. App. 461 (1991) and *Seattle v. Loyd Stalsbroten*, COA#40677-9-I (Div. One May 26, 1998).

Motion is:  granted  _____

denied  _____

reserved  _____

## 15. Implied Element

To dismiss the charges and/or suppress the breath test on the grounds of the State's inability to establish the "Implied Element" of non-consumption of alcohol following the time of driving per *State v. Crediford*, 130 Wash. 2d 747 (1996).

Motion is:  granted  _____

denied  _____

reserved  _____

### 16. Implied Consent Warnings

To suppress the breath test on the grounds of failure to comply with the requirements of RCW 46.20.308 (Implied Consent Warnings).

Motion is:   granted _____

denied   _____

reserved _____

### 17. Implied Consent/Erroneous Warnings

To suppress the breath test results on the grounds that the Implied Consent Warnings read to the defendant were erroneous and inaccurate in that no probationary license is conferred upon minors following a test result of .02 or above, pursuant to *State v. Bartels,* 112 Wash. 2d 882 (1989); *Spokane v. Holmberg,* 50 Wash. App. 317, (1987), *Cooper v. DOL,* 61 Wash. App. 525 (1991).

Motion is:   granted _____

denied   _____

reserved _____

### 18. Implied Consent/Additional Language

To suppress results of the breath test on the grounds of inclusion of additional advisements in violation of the requirements of RCW 46.61.308 and the holdings of *State v. Bartels,* 112 Wash. 2d 882 (1989); *Spokane v. Holmberg,* 50 Wash. App. 317 (1987) and *Cooper v. DOL,* 61 Wash. App. 525 (1991); *State v. Bostrom,* 127 Wash. 2d 580 (1995).

Motion is:   granted _____

denied   _____

reserved _____

### 19. Improper Breath Test Procedure

To suppress the breath test for failure to follow the requirements of the Washington Administrative Code (WAC 448-13 *et seq.*) and the protocols established by the Washington State Toxicologist.

Motion is:   granted _____

denied   _____

reserved _____

### 20. Independent Tests

To dismiss for interference with Defendant's right to obtain an independent test. RCW 46.20.308 and *Blaine v. Suess,* 93 Wash. 2d 722 (1980).

Motion is:  granted    _____
            denied     _____
            reserved   _____

### 21. Simulator Solution
To suppress breath test for failure to comply with the requirements of the Washington Administrative Code (WAC 448.13 *et seq.*) and the protocols established by the Washington State Toxicologist. WAC 448-13.

Motion is:  granted    _____
            denied     _____
            reserved   _____

### 22. Defective Charging Document
To dismiss based on a defective charging document. *Auburn v. Brooke,* 119 Wash. 2d 623 (1992); *State v. Leach,* 113 Wash. 2d 679 (1989); *State v. Kjorsvik,* 117 Wash. 2d 93 (1991).

Motion is:  granted    _____
            denied     _____
            reserved   _____

### 23. Insufficient Evidence
To dismiss for lack of facts sufficient to support a finding of guilt beyond a reasonable doubt of all elements necessary to convict the defendant of the charge(s) pending herein. *State v. Knapstad,* 107 Wash. 2d 346 (1986).

Motion is:  granted    _____
            denied     _____
            reserved   _____

### 24. 3.1 Motion
To dismiss, or in the alternative, suppress based on a violation of the right to counsel based on CrRLJ 3.1.

Motion is:  granted    _____
            denied     _____
            reserved   _____

### 25. Double Jeopardy
Motion to dismiss based on the statute's violation of double jeopardy in violation of Wash. Const. Art. 1, § 9, and U.S. Const. Amend. V.

Motion is:  granted    _____
            denied     _____
            reserved   _____

## II. DISCOVERY MOTIONS

### 1. 911 Tapes, etc.

To compel production of any recording, video tape, or tape recordings, including any radio transmissions between officers and dispatch, between officers, or 911 tapes, or to issue a subpoena duces tecum for same.

Motion is:   granted   _____
             denied    _____
             reserved  _____

### 2. Documentary Materials

To compel disclosure of those evidentiary materials and documents set forth in defendant's Demand for Discovery previously filed herein. CrRLJ 4.7; *State v. Dunnivan,* 65 Wash. App 728 (1992); CrRLJ 4.7(a)(d).

Motion is:   granted   _____
             denied    _____
             reserved  _____

### 3. Police Reports/Field Notes

To compel production of any and all police or investigative reports, including field notes made by the involved officers, and statements of all potential witnesses, including production of *all* documentation of results of physical or mental examinations and/ or scientific tests, experiments, or comparisons made in connection with the charge pending against the Defendant. CrRIJ 4.7 and *State v. Campbell,* 103 Wash. 2d 1 (1984).

Motion is:   granted   _____
             denied    _____
             reserved  _____

### 4. DataMaster Records

To compel production of all documents and records of certifications, evaluations, maintenance, repairs, and telephone complaints for the DataMaster machine in question. RCW 46.61.506(6) and CrRLJ 4.7(d).

Motion is:   granted   _____
             denied    _____
             reserved  _____

### 5. Radio Frequency Interference

To compel disclosure of any information regarding presence of radios, microwaves, short waves, CB's, and any other transmitters or other such devices at or near the location of the DataMaster at the time of the test.

Motion is:    granted    _____

denied    _____

reserved    _____

### 6. Widmark's Formula

To compel disclosure of whether or not the prosecution intends to offer testimony regarding "retrograde extrapolation," or "Widmark's Formula," and, if so, to compel disclosure of the name(s) of the expert witness(es), his/her credentials, qualifications, education, training and experience, and disclosure of any documents, studies, reports, or other materials relied on or material to any aspect of such testimony, and for a summary of their testimony. RCW 46.61.506, CrRLJ 4.7(d).

Motion is:    granted    _____

denied    _____

reserved    _____

### 7. Identity of Experts

To compel disclosure of the identity of the specific breath test technician, simulator solution changer, and state toxicology lab technician the prosecution intends to call at trial, the subject of their testimony, the basis of their expertise, including qualification, education, training and experience, and disclosure of any reports, documents, or studies upon which they intend to rely or make reference to in any aspect of their testimony. CrRLJ 4.7(d).

Motion is:    granted    _____

denied    _____

reserved    _____

### 8. DataMaster Operator's Manual

To compel production of a copy of the BAC Verifier DataMaster Operator's Manual of the officer who administered the breath test, and any manual received or used by the officer who administered field tests, during training for administration of same or for issuance of subpoena duces tecum for said manuals for trial.

Motion is:    granted    _____

denied    _____

reserved    _____

### 9. Subpoena Duces Tecum

For issuance of a Subpoena Duces Tecum directed to the Communications Division, Washington State Patrol Breath Test Section or any other applicable division or person within the Washington State Patrol for production of all records of complaints of malfunctions, operator error, or other communication in the Patrol's possession concerning operation of the BAC Verifier DataMaster used to test the Defendant's breath herein, CrRLJ 4.8(b).

Motion is:  granted  _____

denied  _____

reserved  _____

### 10. Expert/Breath or Blood Test

For discovery of the identity of any state expert witness concerning evidence of the defendant's alleged breath concerning evidence of the defendant's alleged breath or blood alcohol concentration. U.S. Constitution, Fourth and Fourteenth Amendments, Washington Constitution, Art. 1 § 3. *State v. Dunnivan,* 65 Wash. App. 728 (1992), CrRLJ 4.7.

Motion is:  granted  _____

denied  _____

reserved  _____

### 11. Expert Physiological Effects

For discovery of the identity of any state expert witness concerning evidence of the physiological effects of alcohol or any drug on the defendant's ability to operate a motor vehicle. U.S. Constitution, Fourth and Fourteenth Amendments; Washington Constitution, Art. 1 § 3, *State v. Dunnivan,* 65 Wash. App. 728 (1992), CrRLJ 4.7.

Motion is:  granted  _____

denied  _____

reserved  _____

### 12. Expert's Credentials

Defendant requests discovery of the education and training of any expert witness the prosecution intends to offer, both general and specific to the subject of his or her testimony, experience relative to the operation, maintenance, and theory of the instrument used to test the defendant's blood or breath, or simulator solution and a description of the place, date, and subject matter of all training taken by said witnesses regarding the instrument in question or the effects of alcohol or drugs on the human body and a full description of any experiments in which said witnesses have participated or about which he or she may testify, and any documents, studies, reports or other materials relied on or material to any aspect of his or her testimony.

Motion is:  granted  _____
denied  _____
reserved  _____

### 13. Objection to Certificates

Defendant hereby notes an objection to proof of any material fact at hearing or trial by affidavit or certificate. A certified BAC Verifier DataMaster technician *and* the person(s) who conducted any quality assurance tests as well as the person(s) responsible for preparing, storing and installing the simulator solution concerned herein **IS HEREBY DEMANDED AT HEARING OR TRIAL,** including any and all records pertaining to the preparation, checking and installation of the simulator solution used in this case, including the gas chromatograph charts regarding the solution in accordance with CrRLJ 6.13 and RCW 46.61.506(6), along with a copy of his or her permit.

Motion is:  granted  _____
denied  _____
reserved  _____

**IT IS HEREBY ORDERED, ADJUDGED AND DECREED**
that the prosecution shall comply with all granted motions to compel no later than 4 p.m. on the _____ day of _____ , 199__.
**DONE IN OPEN COURT** this _____ day of _____ , 199__.

_____
JUDGE

Presented by:

_____

DOUGLAS COWAN
Attorney for Defendant
WSBA# 2146

# IV

# TRIAL

# 13

# CROSS-EXAMINATION

## §13.0   The Arresting Officer

### §13.0.4   Undermining the Field Sobriety Tests

*Page 926.  Add after fifth full paragraph:*

In considering the defendant's emotional state at the time of the field sobriety tests, the jury should be made clearly aware of the *psycho-physiological effects of anxiety* on test performance. The following materials, provided the author from noted DUI practitioner Steven Oberman of Knoxville, Tennessee,* present the issue clearly:

---

One factor that is not given enough attention, in the opinion of the author, is the role of anxiety on a person's ability to perform the field sobriety tests satisfactorily. This is not discussed in much detail in the NHSTA manuals, but is assumed to have been considered, at least to some extent, in the underlying research for the standardized tests. We may all recall from our schooling that the human autonomic nervous system is divided into two divisions, the sympathetic and the parasympathetic.

An easy way to remember the most important roles of the two autonomic nervous system divisions is to think of the parasympathetic division as the "D" (Digesting, Defecation, and Diuresis

---

*Reprinted with permission.

(Urination)) division, and the sympathitic division as the "E" (Exercise, Excitement, Emergency, and Embarrassment) division.[1]

The sympathetic division is often referred to as the "fight-or-flight" system.[2] Its activity is evident when we are excited or when we find ourselves in an emergency or threatening situation.[3] When this threat or emergency is perceived by the individual, the hypothalamus stimulates the sympathetic fibers as the body prepares for "fight-or-flight."[4] Within a few minutes, the chemicals epinephrine and norepinephrine are released, which cause the anxiety to be manifested through a person's verbal responses, as well as clinical signs, which include perspiration, tremulousness, and rapid pulse and breathing.[5] Equally characteristic are changes in brain wave patterns and in the electrical resistence of the skin (galvanic skin resistence), which are events that are frequently recorded during polygraph examinations.[6] When the body is activated to this "fight-or-flight" status by some short-term stressor or emergency, the sympathetic nervous system is mobilized, causing blood to be diverted from temporarily non-essential organs to the brain, heart, and skeletal muscles.[7] This results in the exhibition of the anxiety symptoms.

Anxiety is a psychological response to stressors that have both physiologic and psychologic components. Anxiety results when a person perceives a threat to the self, either physically or psychogically (such as self-esteem, body image, or identity). The level of anxiety engendered and its manifestations depend on the individual's maturity, understanding of need, level of self-esteem, and coping mechanisisms.[8] The behavioral reactions to anxiety are in-

[1] Elaine N. Marieb, R.N., Ph.D., Human Anatomy and Physiology, 463 (3d ed. 1995).

[2] Elaine N. Marieb, R.N., Ph.D., Human Anatomy and Physiology, 463 (3d ed. 1995).

[3] Elaine N. Marieb, R.N., Ph.D., Human Anatomy and Physiology, 463 (3d ed. 1995).

[4] Judith Haber, Ph.D, RN, CS, FAAN, et al., Comprehensive Psychiatric Nursing, 166 (5th ed. 1997).

[5] Judith Haber, Ph.D, RN, CS, FAAN, et al., Comprehensive Psychiatric Nursing, 166 (5th ed. 1997).

[6] Elaine N. Marieb, R.N., Ph.D., Human Anatomy and Physiology, 463 (3d ed. 1995).

[7] Elaine N. Marieb, R.N., Ph.D., Human Anatomy and Physiology, 570 (3d ed. 1995).

[8] Medical-Surgical Nursing, 172 (Wilma J. Phipps, Ph.D., R.N., FAAN, et al. eds., 5th ed. 1995).

fluenced by psychosocial-cultural factors, basic personality development, past experiences, values, and economic status.[9]

While mild anxiety may result in increased alertness, anxiety can increase to a stage where the subject would suffer from the recognized psychological signs of anxiety such as decreased attention span, decreased ability to follow directions, and increase in the number of questions, and need to seek reassurance.[10] Those who suffer from a severe stress response may actually exhibit immobility.[11] These are the very symptoms that may cause a person who is not under the influence to perform poorly on the standardized field sobriety tests.

Those who regularly practice in the field of DUI defense are aware of officers' frequent testimony that our clients were not acting normally because our client "wanted to fight," "couldn't understand the instructions for the field sobriety tests," "wouldn't shut up," or simply "wouldn't cooperate." In many instances, it is not an intoxicant that causes such behavior from the suspect, but it is rather the suspect's autonomic nervous system response to anxiety resulting from the stressor of the confrontation with the police and fear of going to jail. The changes in bodily functions that provide what the body considers to be optimal physiological conditions in response to the threat of incarceration may be the same factors that convince the officer that the driver is chemically impaired.[12]

## §13.2   Illustrative Cross-Examination of Arresting Officer

### Page 989.  Add at end of section:

The following represents an excellent illustration of an effective cross-examination of the officer, particularly as to field sobri-

---

[9] Medical-Surgical Nursing, 172 (Wilma J. Phipps, Ph.D., R.N., FAAN, et al. eds., 5th ed. 1995).
[10] Medical-Surgical Nursing, 174 (Wilma J. Phipps, Ph.D., R.N., FAAN, et al. eds., 5th ed. 1995).
[11] Medical-Surgical Nursing, 174 (Wilma J. Phipps, Ph.D., R.N., FAAN, et al. eds., 5th ed. 1995).
[12] See Elaine N. Marieb, R.N., Ph.D., Human Anatomy and Physiology, 463 (3d ed. 1995).

ety tests. The examination, modeled largely after the tactics and techniques presented in this book, is the work of noted DUI practitioner Mark Gardner of Cleveland, Ohio.*

### The Polite Lead-In

Q. Officer, if I ask you any question that offends you, or make you feel uncomfortable, please let me know. Will you do that?

A. Yes.

Q. Now, is there any portion of your testimony, where you may have made a mistake, or may have innocently mislead the jury, where in all fairness to you, you now want to correct?

A. No.

### Importance of Not Guessing During Testimony

Q. Now Officer, you understand that this is a criminal trial, don't you?

A. Yes.

Q. And you understand the seriousness of the charge you've leveled against my client?

A. Yes.

Q. And because these charges are so serious, are you willing to promise now, before this jury, that you're going to testify to those things that you are 100 percent sure about?

A. Yes.

Q. So that you will not be guessing, or speculating or making any inferences. You are only going to testify to those things that you know for certain?

A. Yes.

### Cop's Prior Experience at Testifying (Very Optional)

Q. Now, from looking at your uniform, it is obvious that you are a police officer. Correct?

A. Yes.

Q. And it is true that you attended a police academy or training school before you were allowed to become a police officer?

A. Yes.

Q. And at that academy, you studied a number of different subjects?

*Reprinted with permission.

*A.* Yes.

*Q.* And one of those subjects was how to testify?

*A.* I believe so.

*Q.* In fact, the course was how to testify convincingly so as to get the jury to believe you?

*A.* [Who cares what his answer is.]

*Q.* And part of this training was how to anticipate certain questions?

*A.* [Who cares what his answer is.]

*Q.* And how to respond to certain answers?

*A.* [Who care what his answer is.]

*Q.* In fact, you were trained in a classroom setting how to present yourself as a believable-sounding witness?

*A.* [Who cares what his answer is.]

*Q.* Do you agree that your demeanor on the stand today is more polished then when you first started testifying?

*A.* [Who cares what his answer is.]

*Q.* And that's because you have had experience at testifying?

*A.* [Who cares.]


*Cop's Memory of Events*

*Q.* Is the night you arrested my client the first time you ever met him?

*A.* Yes.

*Q.* You did prepare an arrest report for your arrest of D?

*A.* Yes.

*Q.* I assume your report was prepared at around the time of your contact with my client as well as shortly thereafter?

*A.* Yes.

*Q.* Prior to testifying today, have you had an opportunity to review this report?

*A.* Yes.

*Q.* Has reading this report refreshed your memory, or do you need more time to review it?

*A.* I remember it well.

*Q.* Now concerning your memory, would you agree that your memory of the events that occurred that night were better at the time that you wrote the report than now, some three months later?

*A.* Maybe a bit.

*Q.* Well, could you tell me the average number of persons you ticket monthly?

*A.* Twenty.

*Q.* How about the number of persons you arrest for DUI?

*A.*  Four.

*Q.*  How about the name of the person you ticketed before you arrested D?

*A.*  I don't recall.

*Q.*  How about the name of the person you ticketed after D?

*A.*  I don't recall.

*Q.*  How about the name of the person you arrested for DUI before you arrested D?

*A.*  Don't recall.

*Q.*  How about the name of the person you arrested for DUI after you arrested D?

*A.*  Don't recall.

*Q.*  How about the total number of tickets written since you arrested D?

*A.*  Don't know.

*Q.*  How about the total number of DUI arrests since you arrested D?

*A.*  Don't recall.

*Q.*  Officer, will you admit to this jury that you have forgotten things in the past?

*A.*  Sometimes.

*Q.*  Will you also admit to this jury that you have sometimes incorrectly remembered some events in the past?

*A.*  Rarely.

*Q.*  Officer, isn't it a fact that you sometimes mix up the facts of one case with those of another case?

*A.*  [Who cares what his answer is.]

## If cop appears to be guessing as to anything, ask the following

*Q.*  Is it true that you are just as sure about _____ as you are about my client being under the influence?

*A.*  [Who cares what his answer is.]


*Duty to Accurately Complete the Arrest Report*

*Q.*  Now concerning your report, you were taught at the police academy the reasons for filling out an arrest report, weren't you?

*A.*  Yes.

*Q.*  You were taught that you must fully and accurately complete the report so that, if a trial takes place some months after the arrest, you would be able to remember the details of the arrest, is this correct?

*A.*  Yes.

*Q.*  And the reason for this is that you were taught that observational evidence — first, could you explain to the jury what observations evidence is?

A. Blah, blah, blah.

Q. You were taught at the academy that observation evidence is short-lived evidence?

A. Yes.

Q. Another reason for fully completing this form is that the state's attorney may review your arrest report, evaluate the case, and develop an appropriate strategy to get a conviction?

A. Yes.

Q. At the academy, you were taught to include all significant and material information in your report?

A. Yes.

Q. When you reviewed your report, did you note any inaccuracies? Is there anything in the report you wish to change some three months after writing it?

A. No.

Q. Then may I presume that you properly discharged your duty and carefully and completely recorded all significant aspects of what you observed?

A. Yes.

Q. Then, after reviewing your report this morning, are you now going to testify that you omitted any information that you should have included in your report?

A. No.


*Length of Time Before Writing Report (Very Optional)*

Q. Now about this arrest report — you wrote it at the police station?

A. Yes.

Q. So that means you wrote your report sometime after pulling D over on the road, is that correct?

A. Yes.

Q. And that you wrote your report sometime after D exited his vehicle?

A. Yes.

Q. And your report was written after you asked D to perform the various coordination and balance exercises?

A. Yes.

Q. And it was written after you had already made up your mind as to how D performed on these exercises?

A. Yes.

Q. And it was written after, in your opinion, you were dissatisfied with how D performed on these exercises?

A.   Yes.

Q.   In fact, you wrote your report after D was placed under arrest?

A.   Yes.

Q.   And it was written after you placed D in handcuffs?

A.   Yes.

Q.   And you wrote it after you had called various information back to dispatch?

A.   Yes.

Q.   And still after a tow truck had been called by dispatch?

A.   Yes.

Q.   In fact, you wrote your report after the tow truck arrived on scene?

A.   Yes.

Q.   And it was written after the tow truck towed away D's car?

A.   Yes.

Q.   In fact, it was written sometime after you arrived back at the station with D in the back seat?

A.   Yes.

Q.   Now, one of the first things you did upon arriving at the station with D was read D his rights, correct?

A.   Yes.

Q.   So you were taking care of business other than writing your report at this time?

A.   Yes.

Q.   And at some point, you read D something called the Implied Consent Law?

A.   Yes.

Q.   And again, that was prior to you sitting down and writing your arrest report?

A.   Yes.

Q.   All told, you finally sat down to write out your report some two hours after you pulled D over and arrested him?

A.   Yes.

Q.   So you wrote your report out in a manner that would tend to justify your actions in arresting D?

A.   I wrote down what I witnessed.


*Selectivity of Report/Cop's Predisposition to Slant Report*

Q.   Officer, I believe you testified earlier that in writing out your report, you were careful and complete in recording all significant and material aspects of what you observed. Is that correct?

A.   Yes, that's true.

*Q.* Would you consider information tending to prove D innocent as "significant" and "material?"

*A.* I would guess so.

*Q.* Then is it fair to say that you included in your report observation tending to prove D was not intoxicated? That the charges you filed against him may be wrong?

*A.* I'm not sure what you mean.

*Q.* Well, did you write down in your report that it took D an extremely long time to pull his car over to the side of the road after you activated your overhead lights and siren?

*A.* No.

*Q.* Would you please check your report to make sure of this?

*A.* No, I did not write that down.

*Q.* Is it safe to assume that you did not write this information in your report because D pulled his car over within a normal amount of time?

*A.* I guess so.

*Q.* If D had driven on for miles after you activated your lights and siren, completely ignoring your order to pull over, would you have written that in your report?

*A.* Yes.

*Q.* And you would have written that information because it is both significant and material?

*A.* Yes.

*Q.* In fact, you would have treated that as an indication that the amount of alcohol D had consumed had affected his ability to both observe and respond to your commands, correct?

*A.* Yes.

*Q.* Now, people who are driving drunk, they have problems with dividing their attentions, correct?

*A.* Yes.

*Q.* For instance, they can focus on what's happening straight in front of them, but they won't notice sirens and strobe lights flashing behind them?

*A.* That's correct.

*Q.* So, taking an unreasonably long time to pull your car over after being signaled to by a police officer is a common phenomenon associated with intoxicated drivers, is it not?

*A.* Yes.

*Q.* Then the opposite must be true. Pulling your car over within a reasonable amount of time is at least one sign that the driver of this vehicle is capable of properly dividing his attention, and is not intoxicated. His mind and body were responding in the same manner as a sober and law-abiding person's mind and body would respond?

A. Some drunk people pull over fast, too.

Q. Well, the truth of the matter is, you did not write in your report a fact that proves that D was able to control his car in a fashion consistent with a perfectly sober person? Then his driving ability was not affected?

A. Like I said, that's not conclusive proof that he was sober.

Q. But the fact is, my client's actions, reactions, and mental processes were functioning in a manner consistent with a sober person?

A. I guess so.

Q. Did you write in your report that when D pulled his car over, he slammed on his brakes, or almost drove off the road, or left half of his car on the road instead of pulling it onto the shoulder?

A. No.

Q. Would you please check your report to make sure of that?

A. As I said, I did not write that in my report.

Q. If he would have done any of these things, is there any question in your mind that you would have written that in your report as proof that, in your opinion, D was too intoxicated to properly operate his car?

A. I probably would have.

Q. Is it safe to assume that because you did not write in your report that D did any of these things, that in fact, D pulled over his car in a safe and reasonable manner?

A. I guess so.

Q. Now, people who are driving drunk, they have problems with their fine motor skills, is that correct?

A. Yes.

Q. For instance, problems steering, braking, judging distance?

A. Yes.

Q. So, pulling your car over in an unsafe and reckless manner is a common phenomenon associated with intoxicated drivers, is it not?

A. Yes.

Q. Then, once again, the opposite must be true. Pulling your car over in a safe and reasonable manner is another sign that D was not intoxicated. In fact, my client's actions, reactions, and mental processes responded in the same way a sober person's would have responded?

A. As I said before, that is not proof that D was sober.

Q. Now, you've testified at an earlier hearing that when you arrested my client, you read him his Miranda rights?

A. Yes.

*Q.* There are four or five sentences that comprise the Miranda rights that you are required to read to individuals you arrest, correct?

*A.* Yes.

*Q.* You read them from a card you probably have right now in your wallet or shirt pocket?

*A.* Yes.

*Q.* And your testimony is that my client waived his Miranda rights and agreed to talk to you without an attorney present?

*A.* Yes.

*Q.* And he did speak with you, and answered your questions?

*A.* Yes.

*Q.* From your police training, you understand, do you not, that for a Miranda waiver to be effective, the person waiving them must fully understand exactly what his Miranda rights are?

*A.* Yes.

*Q.* And that he can only waive his Miranda rights by making a knowing, intelligent, and voluntary decision to give up those rights?

*A.* Yes.

*Q.* Officer, did you violate my client's constitutional Miranda rights on the night you arrested him?

*A.* No.

*Q.* Are you saying then that you feel confident that my client made a knowing, intelligent, and voluntary waiver of his Miranda rights?

*A.* Yes.

*Q.* And you're saying that my client understood these rights?

*A.* Yes.

*Q.* And you're saying that my client waived these rights?

*A.* Yes.

*Q.* And you understood my client's response, that he was willing to waive these rights?

*A.* Yes.

(Probably don't ask this question — save for argument)

*Q.* Then you are telling this jury that whatever amount of alcohol my client consumed — whether mild or potent — did not affect his normal mental processes. His ability to comprehend his rights and make an intelligent decision was not impaired by any alcohol?

*A.* Not much.

*Q.* Isn't it true that in your report, you only wrote down information that supports yourself, information that puts another DUI arrest under your belt?

*A.* I wrote down what I believed to be important.

*Q.* So, facts that would tend to show that D is innocent — that he did not violate the law — that information is not important to you?

*A.* I wrote down what I considered to be good evidence.

*Q.* Well, seeing as you needed to read your report to remember what happened, and in your report you only wrote down your opinions that tend to make D look guilty, aren't you testifying as to only a portion of what happened? Only that part that brings you a step closer to making Sergeant?

*A.* I'm trying to tell you what I saw.

On the other hand, if the cop tries to add facts not written in his report

*Q.* Officer, you just testified that D failed to pull over in a reasonable and safe manner?

*A.* Correct.

*Q.* Now, pulling over in an unsafe fashion is pretty significant and material in a drunk driving case, isn't it?

*A.* Yes.

*Q.* And you have testified that you were trained to record in your report all significant and material observations?

*A.* Yes.

*Q.* And you have testified that the reason you record these observations is because observational evidence is short-lived?

*A.* Yes.

*Q.* And you also testified earlier that you properly discharged your duty and carefully and completely recorded all significant aspects of what you observed?

*A.* Yes.

*Q.* You also testified earlier that there were no omissions in your report?

*A.* Yes.

*Q.* In fact, you even swore under oath that "you are not now going to testify that you omitted any information that you should have included in your report."

*A.* Yes.

*Q.* So what you previously swore to under oath wasn't exactly accurate and true?

*A.* [Who cares.]

*D's Scared/Fragile/Embarrassed Mental Condition*

*Q.* You pulled D's car over at around two o'clock in the morning?

*A.* Yes.

Q. Is it your experience that citizens that you pull over are somewhat nervous and scared at being pulled over?

A. Not always.

Q. But the vast majority of the time, they are embarrassed?

A. Yes.

Q. Distressed quite a bit?

A. Yes.

Q. Tense?

A. Sometimes.

Q. And this is how the average citizen appears when talking to you while sitting in the driver's seat and you outside his car?

A. Yes.

Q. Well, in this case, you ordered D to get out of his car because you believed he was DUI, is that correct?

A. Yes.

Q. Certainly, the prospect of being arrested and jailed must have made D quite scared?

A. I would guess so.

Q. Embarrassed.

A. Probably.

Q. Nervous, tense?

A. Probably.

*Preliminary Questions Cop Should Ask D*

Q. There came a point in time where you asked D to step out of the car?

A. Yes.

Q. The purpose of that was to have D perform various coordination and dexterity exercises, which you like to call sobriety tests?

A. Yes.

Q. Will you agree with me that as individuals, people differ substantially in their abilities, skills, and talents?

A. Yes.

Q. People do have different athletic abilities?

A. Yes.

Q. And all people do not have the same coordination and balance skills, do they? I mean, we've both seen people in circuses that can walk tightrope wires one hundred feet up in the air. You and I can't do that, can we?

A. I know I can't.

Q. In your opinion, would it be important to know about any physical limitations that D has, prior to asking him to perform these exercises?

*A.* It could help.

*Q.* Okay, so let's talk about some of the things that can affect a person's ability to perform balance and coordination exercises.

*A.* Okay.

*Q.* How about a painful back? Would a painful back likely affect a person's performance of these coordination and balance exercises?

*A.* I guess it could have an impact.

*Q.* How about knee problems?

*A.* Yes. But D never told me that he had any physical problems or injuries.

*Q.* Did you ask D if he had any injuries before you had him start these exercises?

*A.* No.

*Q.* Didn't you just testify that you wanted to be fair to D, that he had a fair opportunity to perform these exercises to your satisfaction?

*A.* Yes. And I did give him a fair opportunity to pass the sobriety tests.

*Q.* But you never bothered to ask him if he had an injury or other problems that would hinder him in performing your exercises?

*A.* No.

*Q.* Never asked him about sore joints or arthritis?

*A.* No.

*Q.* Wouldn't that sort of information have been relevant in judging how D performed the coordination and balance exercises?

*A.* Maybe just a bit.

*Q.* But you never did bother to ask these few simple questions that could have helped you form a more intelligent and informed opinion about D?

*A.* No.

*Q.* Would you agree with me that if D had any of the physical ailments that we just discussed, that judging D by how he performed on these difficult exercises is a bit unfair?

*A.* Maybe. But as I said, D didn't tell me had had any physical problems.

*Q.* You know, of course, that a person's balance is determined in large part by the fluid in his inner ear?

*A.* I believe that is true.

*Q.* But you didn't bother to ask D if he had a cold, did you?

*A.* No.

*Q.* You didn't ask him if he had sinus congestion?

*A.* No.

*Q.* Didn't ask him if he was taking medication for his sinuses, did you?

*A.* No.

*Q.* Did you ask him if he was taking an over-the-counter medication for any illnesses or injuries?

*A.*   No.

*Q.*   Do you know if he was taking over-the-counter medications?

*A.*   No.

*Q.*   If he was taking over-the-counter medications, can it be that these perfectly legal, everyday medications were what caused D to have performed the coordination and balancing exercises the way he did?

*A.*   I don't know.

*Q.*   You don't know, because you never bothered to ask D if he was taking over-the-counter medications?

*A.*   I guess so.

*Q.*   And the same holds true for any prescription medicines D was taking. You have no way of ruling out his prescription medications as the cause of how D performed on these exercises, do you?

*A.*   No.

*Q.*   Now, you are a police officer, aren't you?

*A.*   Yes.

*Q.*   When you stopped D, you were investigating the possibility of a drunk driver on the road?

*A.*   Yes.

*Q.*   Are you telling this jury that your investigations are only concerned with technicalities that tend to make people look guilty, but that you ignore investigating details that may prove that people are innocent?

*A.*   No. That's not what I'm saying.

*Q.*   But the fact is, you never bothered to ask D a few simple questions about his physical condition?

*A.*   No.

*Q.*   Well, the fact of the matter is, you're here trying to get D convicted of a very serious crime based on both your opinion and a half-completed investigation. Isn't that so?

*A.*   I'm telling you what I believe is true.

*Q.*   Okay, before you stopped D, how long had he been driving for?

*A.*   I don't know.

*Q.*   Well, isn't it a common phenomenon to be rather stiff, and have poor lower body circulation, after having sat in the same position for long periods of time?

*A.*   Sometimes.

*Q.*   When you told D to perform these exercises, did you tell him to walk around a bit to get any stiffness out of his joints, or to get his blood circulating?

*A.*   No.

*Q.* Would that have been a little more fair to D to give him the opportunity to move around a bit before giving him these exercises?

*A.* I really don't think that it matters.

*Q.* According to your report, you pulled D over at around two o'clock in the morning.

*A.* Yes.

*Q.* Do you know for how many hours D had been up that day?

*A.* No. I didn't ask him that.

*Q.* Didn't you think that was an important fact to know?

*A.* No. Not really.

*Q.* Well, let me ask you this hypothetical. There are two people. Both have no alcohol or drugs in their body. The first person has worked a long day, he's been up for 18 hours and is exhausted. The second person has been up for five hours and is well rested. It is your opinion, under oath, that the first person is likely to perform these exercises as well as the second person?

*A.* The sobriety tests are designed so that anyone can pass them.

*Q.* So, you're telling this jury under oath, that the first person should be able to do every bit as good on your exercises as the second person?

*A.* Maybe not as good, but good enough to pass.

*Q.* Isn't it a fact that you conducted this investigation with the view of making D look guilty? You were not interested in D's innocence, were you?

*A.* That's not right.

*Q.* But the fact is, you didn't ask a couple of simple questions that would have helped you make a more intelligent and informed decision?

*A.* I just forgot to ask a couple of questions.


*When Probable Cause Arose (the Sobriety Test "Lock")*

*Q.* Now, you've already testified as to how D was driving that night. Correct?

*A.* Yes.

*Q.* You didn't arrest him for driving DUI as soon as you pulled him over, did you?

*A.* No.

*Q.* And the reason why is because, based on his driving alone, you had not formed the opinion that D was intoxicated?

*A.* Correct.

*Q.* And that means you did not believe that you had probable cause to arrest D for DUI?

*A.* Correct.

*Q.* Now, you've testified about a number of observations you made of the defendant upon pulling him over. Specifically, you told this jury about a slurred speech, a strong odor of an alcoholic beverage, disheveled appearance and eyes that were bloodshot and glassy.

*A.* That's correct.

*Q.* Did you arrest D for DUI upon making these observations?

*A.* No.

*Q.* And again, that is because, in your opinion, you had not yet formed the opinion that my client was intoxicated?

*A.* Not at that point.

*Q.* And because you weren't sure at that point, you correctly determined that you did not have probable cause to arrest him for DUI?

*A.* Correct.

*Q.* Now building upon that point, you had D step out of his car. Correct?

*A.* Yes.

*Q.* And you say that he had stumbled getting out of the car, and that he had to lean against the car door to maintain his balance?

*A.* Correct.

*Q.* Again, you did not arrest him at this point?

*A.* Correct.

*Q.* And the reason that you didn't arrest him for DUI at this point is that you still had not yet formed opinion that my client was intoxicated?

*A.* I wanted more information on which to base my decision.

*Q.* And because you didn't have all the information you needed to determine if my client was intoxicated, you correctly decided that you did not have probable cause to arrest him for DUI?

*A.* Correct.

*Q.* And that is why you wanted to administer what you called "field sobriety tests"?

*A.* Correct.

*Q.* Because to reach "probable cause" of intoxication, you need to have my client perform certain balance and coordination exercises?

*A.* Yes.

*Q.* And without having my client perform these physical tests, today, in front of this jury, you stand by your decision you made on this particular night. That based just upon your observations of my client's driving and his appearance, and how he spoke and how he smelled, you did not have probably cause to arrest him for DUI?

*A.* I guess so.

*Q.* So your "probable cause" to arrest D for drunk driving was based on how he performed on these "field sobriety tests"?

*A.* Yes.

*Q.* And these exercises were all important to you in forming your opinion as to whether D was driving intoxicated?

*A.* Yes.

*Q.* So if D had performed the coordination and balance exercises to your satisfaction, that means that you would not have arrested D. Is that correct?

*A.* Correct.

*Q.* Now, in having D perform your tests, you were trying to be as fair as possible to D, were you not?

*A.* I was.

*Q.* The first test you gave D was the HGN. Is that correct?

*A.* Yes.

*Q.* The next test was the Walk and Turn?

*A.* Yes.

*Q.* The last test was the one-leg stand?

*A.* Yes.

*Q.* You evaluated D on how he performed on each test?

*A.* Yes.

*Q.* You formed an opinion as to how D performed each test?

*A.* Yes.

*Q.* You were sure not to make any quick or snap decisions as to how D performed these tests?

*A.* Yes.

*Q.* After D performed the HGN, you did not arrest him for DUI at that point. Did you?

*A.* Not at that point.

*Q.* And the reason for that is that you had not yet completed your investigation?

*A.* Correct.

*Q.* You wanted additional information?

*A.* Correct.

*Q.* In fairness to D, you wanted additional information to base our decision of intoxication or not?

*A.* Correct.

*Q.* And that is because you still had doubt about D being DUI after the HGN?

*A.* I was trying to be open-minded, out of fairness to your client.

*Q.* Okay. You were open-minded as to whether my client was intoxicated or not after he performed the HGN. Correct?

*A.* Correct.

Q. And you were still open-minded as to whether my client was intoxicated or not after he performed the Walk and Turn. Correct?

A. Correct.

Q. And it was only after the one-leg stand that you made up your mind and decided that you had probable cause to arrest my client for DUI. Correct?

A. Correct.

Q. Okay. So it was only after the one-leg stand was complete did you form the opinion that you had probable cause to arrest D for DUI?

A. That's correct.

*Odor of Alcohol*

Q. You testified earlier to smelling the "strong odor of alcohol" about my client. Is that correct?

A. Yes.

Q. And the inference that you're trying to make is that a "strong odor of alcohol" somehow relates to a person who is intoxicated?

A. I believe so.

Q. Isn't it true, and haven't you been taught, that alcohol has no odor? Rather, that it's the beverage that the alcohol is in, and not the alcohol, that creates the odor?

A. True.

Q. Well, from this strong odor you say you smelled, could you tell the jury what type of beverage D had drank?

A. I believe it was beer.

Q. Did you write this down in your report?

A. No.

Q. From the odor, could you tell where D had consumed the beverage?

A. No.

Q. Could you tell when D had consumed the beverage?

A. No.

Q. Could you tell how much or how little of the beverage that D had consumed?

A. No.

*Slurred Speech*

Q. During the course of your investigation, you spoke with my client?

A. Yes.

Q. And from what you've testified to, my client spoke back to you. Correct?

A. Yes.

Q.   In fact, my client spoke hundreds of words to you on that night?
A.   Maybe.
Q.   Could you tell us one word that my client said in a slurred manner?
A.   No [leave it at that]

Or

A.   Yes.
Q.   Then can you tell us what word it is that my client slurred?
A.   Blah, blah, blah.
Q.   Can you demonstrate for the jury exactly how he slurred that word?
A.   Blah, blah, blah.
Q.   Isn't it true that on every DUI arrest you make, you always say that the suspect slurs his words?
A.   [Who cares what his answer is.]

*Specific Instructions Given to D*

Q.   You've testified that you have made numerous arrests for DUI throughout your career, is that correct?
A.   Yes.
Q.   And that means that you have given the instructions to perform the coordination and balance exercises many times?
A.   Yes.
Q.   I'm holding in my hand a tape recorder. What I would like you to do is to repeat the instructions to the exercises that you gave to D, and that I assume you gave to all the other people you arrested for DUI.
A.   Right now?
Q.   Yes. And please, I want you to say it just like you did on the evening you arrested D.
A.   Blah, blah, blah.
Counsel:   Your Honor, I wish to mark the recording just made by Officer Bullethead as Defendant's Exhibit 1.
Judge:   It will be marked as such.

*Test Site Conditions*

Q.   You pulled D over off to the side of the highway?
A.   Yes.
Q.   Is this where you administered the coordination and balance exercises?
A.   Yes.

*Q.* At two o'clock in the morning?

*A.* Yes.

*Q.* The highway where you pulled D over is not a lighted highway, is it?

*A.* No.

*Q.* According to the ticket your wrote, you say that there was moderate traffic driving on the highway at the time?

*A.* Yes.

*Q.* And that the traffic was in both the oncoming and same-direction lanes?

*A.* Yes.

*Q.* The speed limit on the highway is 55 mph?

*A.* Yes.

*Q.* And being as it was late at night, these cars must have had their headlights on?

*A.* I assume so.

*Q.* So the headlights of cars whizzing by were in D's eyes as he was trying to perform your exercises?

*A.* I guess so.

*Q.* And the pressure waves of these 55-mph cars were also hitting D as he was trying to balance himself?

*A.* I don't believe they affected him.

*Q.* Is it possible that any of these cars that were passing you and D were exceeding the speed limit? Could you tell if any of the cars were doing, say 75 mph?

*A.* I couldn't tell.

*Q.* With all these cars driving by, were you at all afraid of being rear-ended?

*A.* It's always a concern.

*Q.* Did you have the overhead lights of your cruiser on, as a way of notifying other drivers that you were pulled over?

*A.* Yes.

*Q.* The overhead lights that you're talking about are the red and blue flashing lights?

*A.* Yes.

*Q.* Both strobes and halogen lights flashing?

*A.* Yes.

*Q.* So the red and blue flashing lights were also in D's face while he was trying to perform the exercises?

*A.* Well, yes. But it didn't affect him.

*Q.* Did you notice his footwear?

*A.* I believe he was wearing sneakers.

*Q.* Sneakers have soft soles, don't they? I mean they're softer than your normal dress shoe?

*A.* Yes.

*Q.* You had D perform the exercises on the shoulder of the highway?

*A.* Yes.

*Q.* It it safe to assume that this highway shoulder is just like every other highway shoulder in this state, covered with small pebbles and gravel?

*A.* No. Actually, it was clear.

*Q.* Okay, so this small strip of highway is very unique within this state. It has no pebbles, gravel, or other small obstructions. Well, is it then like every other highway shoulder in this state in that it slopes down away from the highway for drainage purposes?

*A.* I didn't notice any sloping.

*Q.* And, as you said earlier, D did appear to be a little nervous and embarrassed.

*A.* Yes.

*Q.* Okay, D had to perform these difficult exercises under these unique conditions, or else you were going to say that D was drunk and arrest him?

*A.* Yes.

*Q.* And under these circumstances, D had to perform various coordination and balance exercises?

*A.* Yes.

*Q.* Are these conditions we just spoke about fair to D?

*A.* I believe that a sober person should have been able to perform the sobriety tests properly under these conditions.

*Q.* Fair enough that you would have a member of this jury perform them under the same conditions if you pulled one of them over?

*A.* Yes.

*Q.* And if one of the jurors paused while performing the Walk and Turn, or put his foot down during the one-leg stand, you would also arrest them for drunk driving?

*A.* If I believed they were intoxicated, yes.

*Q.* You've testified that you have been a cop for the past eight years. Is that correct?

*A.* Yes.

*Q.* During that time, you have written hundreds, maybe thousands of traffic tickets?

*A.* Yes.

*Q.* A lot of these tickets have been written to individuals pulled over on the side of the road?

*A.* Yes.

*Q.* Is it fair to say that you've become pretty used to standing on the side of a busy freeway with cars whizzing by at 60 mph?

*A.* I'd say so.

*Q.* How long did it take you to get used to that?

*A.* Not long.

*Q.* Longer than you gave my client to get used to it?

*A.* [Who cares what his answer is.]

*Q.* Tell me, after you arrested D, you took him back to the police station?

*A.* Yes.

*Q.* Are there other officers at the station?

*A.* Yes.

*Q.* You had him sit across a table from you as you filled out various paperwork?

*A.* Yes.

*Q.* Was this room lighted?

*A.* Yes.

*Q.* Nice bright fluorescent lights?

*A.* Yes.

*Q.* Was the floor covered with tiling?

*A.* Yes.

*Q.* I take it the tiled floor is flat and smooth?

*A.* Yes.

*Q.* Is it also true that there are no wind gusts in this room?

*A.* Yes.

*Q.* This room's temperature is just right; not too cold, not too hot?

*A.* Yes.

*Q.* In other words, all the environmental conditions were as good as they could be in the booking room?

*A.* I guess so.

*Q.* These conditions were a lot better than what my client had to put up with on the highway when you had him do the exercises.

*A.* I told you: I don't think any of that affected how he performed.

*Q.* Would it have been at all possible for you to allow D to repeat any of these exercises under fair and decent conditions?

*A.* I guess I could have.

*Q.* But you absolutely, positively did not allow D the opportunity to perform your exercises at the station under optimal conditions?

*A.* No.

*Q.* And it is not your practice to allow people you arrest for DUI to perform the exercises at the station?

*A.* No, it's not.

*Q.* Have you ever performed any of these same exercises?

*A.*  Yes. When I went through DUI training school.

*Q.*  I take it the training class was conducted in a classroom setting?

*A.*  Yes.

*Q.*  Have you ever performed these exercises under circumstances other than for training purposes?

*A.*  No.

*Q.*  Then you don't know what it feels like to perform these exercises when you're nervous?

*A.*  No.

*Q.*  When you're embarrassed?

*A.*  No.

*Q.*  Under a lot of stress?

*A.*  No.

*Q.*  In short, you've never performed these exercises in a suspect situation?

*A.*  No.


*Was D Told What He Would Be Graded On?*

*Q.*  You've already told us specific instructions you gave D regarding each test, is that correct?

*A.*  Yes.

*Q.*  Considering the Walk and Turn, did you tell D that if he started before you finished giving the instructions it would count against him?

*A.*  No.

*Q.*  And you didn't tell him that raising his arms even a little bit was going to be counted against him?

*A.*  No.

*Q.*  In fact, you never told him anything about what he was going to be graded on, did you?

*A.*  I gave him instructions and he had to follow them.

*Q.*  You're not answering my question. You never told him what he was going to be graded on, did you?

*A.*  No.

*Q.*  You gave D what you want to call a "test," but you never told him what he was going to be graded on?

*A.*  Yes.

*Q.*  Does it strike you as fair that you "failed" D on parts of the exercises that he had no way of knowing he was being graded on?

*A.*  Like I said, I gave him instructions and he had to follow them.

*Q.*  Could you have told D what you were going to grade him on?

*A.*  Yes.

*Q.* But you didn't?

*A.* That's not how I was taught to do it.

*Q.* Isn't it true that if you told more people what they were going to be graded on, that more people would do better on these exercises?

*A.* Maybe.


## HORIZONTAL GAZE NYSTAGMUS (HGN)

*Lack of Officer's Qualifications/Understanding of HGN*

*Q.* One of the so-called "tests" you say you performed on D was the Horizontal Gaze Nystagmus?

*A.* Yes.

*Q.* Are you claiming to be an expert in diagnosing and interpreting the medical conditions of human eyes?

*A.* I was taught to detect the nystagmus related to alcohol consumption.

*Q.* Please tell the jury the name of the doctor who taught you how to diagnose the various conditions of the human eyes?

*A.* I wasn't taught by a doctor.

*Q.* The fact is, you were taught by another police officer?

*A.* Yes.

*Q.* And that police officer wasn't a doctor, was he?

*A.* I don't know.

*Q.* Well, if he was a doctor, he sure didn't claim to be one, did he?

*A.* No.

*Q.* And you didn't address him as doctor, did you?

*A.* No.

*Q.* Of course, you don't hold any degrees in the field of medicine or human physiology, do you?

*A.* No.

*Q.* You don't have any licenses related to the practice of medicine or human physiology?

*A.* No.

*Q.* No higher studies in the fields of ophthalmology, or neurology or pharmacology?

*A.* No.

*Q.* But you feel certain that you can medically diagnose ocular nystagmus?

*A.* Yes.

*Q.* Please explain to the jury how, in your mind, alcohol causes nystagmus?

*A.* I don't know. I was just taught that it did.

*Q.* [Having a medical dictionary nearby] Could you explain to the jury the difference between Nystagmus and Saccadic Intrusions?

*A.* No.

*Q.* Do you know what a Saccadic Intrusion is?

*A.* No.

*Q.* Could you please read from this medical dictionary the definition of a Saccadic Intrusion?

*A.* Blah, blah, blah.

*Q.* Now, please explain to the jury the differences between Nystagmus and Saccadic Intrusion?

*A.* I don't know.

*Q.* [Still with the medical dictionary nearby] Then could you explain to the jury the differences between Nystagmus and Saccadic Ocular Oscillations and Oscillopsia?

*A.* No.

*Q.* Could you please read from this medical dictionary the definitions of Saccadic Ocular Oscillations and Oscillopsia?

*A.* Blah, blah, blah.

*Q.* Now, having just read the definitions, please explain to the jury the differences between Nystagmus and Saccadic Ocular Oscillations and Oscillopsia?

*A.* I can't.

*Q.* So what you're saying is, that you have no idea what Saccadic Intrusions and Ocular Oscillations look like?

*A.* Yes.

*HGN Option #1*

*Q.* Now, concerning Nystagmus — have you ever heard of Acquired Fixation Nystagmus?

*A.* No.

*Q.* I take it then that if you've never heard of it, you do not know what it looks like?

*A.* Correct.

*Q.* Well, if you don't know what it looks like, how do you know that what you actually saw was Acquired Fixation Nystagmus?

*A.* I guess I don't.

*Q.* Have you ever heard of Anticipatory Induced Nystagmus?

*A.* No.

*Q.* I take it then that if you've never heard of it, you do not know what it looks like?

*A.* Correct.

*Q.* Well, if you don't know what it looks like, how do you know that what you actually saw was Anticipatory Induced Nystagmus?

*A.* I guess I don't.

[If the attorney wishes to truly punish the testifying cop, run all 47 different types of Nystagmus through the same three monotonous questions. Of course, the same thing can be done for the 16 different types of Saccadic Intrusions and Oscillations.]

*HGN Option #2*

*Q.* Officer, are you aware of how many different types of nystagmus and saccadic intrusions there are?

*A.* Not exactly. I heard there were a lot.

*Q.* I'm going to read to you just some of the different types of nystagmus and saccadic intrusions. Please tell me if you have heard of any of them. OK?

*A.* Yes.

[Read as many of them as you like.]

*Q.* You don't recognize any of the ones I've just read?

*A.* No.

*Q.* The reason you don't recognize any of them is that you're not an eye doctor. Correct?

*A.* Yes.

*Q.* You can't explain to the jury what the causes of these conditions are?

*A.* No.

*Q.* Or what brings them on?

*A.* No.

*Q.* Or even how they look?

*A.* No.

*Q.* You don't know if any of these conditions look exactly like what you're calling HGN?

*A.* I know what I was taught.

*Q.* Please answer my question. You don't know if any of these conditions look exactly like what you're calling HGN?

*A.* I guess not.

*Administration of the HGN to the Defendant*

*Q.* You were taught, were you not, that to administer this examination, the subject must keep his head still and follow an object only with his eyes. Is that correct?

*A.* Yes.

157

Q.  And it takes approximately one-and-a-half minutes to conduct this examination?

A.  Yes.

Q.  And you believe you performed this procedure correctly?

A.  Yes.

Q.  Well, didn't you write in your report and testify that D was extremely impaired?

A.  Yes.

Q.  That he couldn't keep his balance?

A.  Yes.

Q.  That he was staggering?

A.  Yes.

Q.  That he was swaying?

A.  Yes.

Q.  And that this condition persisted from the time you first observed D until the time you turned him over to the jailer?

A.  Yes.

Q.  So your testimony now is that for about two hours, D could and didn't stop swaying, staggering, and stumbling, except for one-and-a-half minutes during which time he kept his body and head perfectly still?

A.  Yes.

Q.  You administered the HGN out on the highway?

A.  Yes.

Q.  You testified earlier that you had your overhead lights on, as well?

A.  Yes. They were on.

Q.  By your overheads, we're talking about your red and blue flashing strobe lights and halogen lights?

A.  Yes.

Q.  Now, these lights are designed to be seen by others from miles away, correct?

A.  Yes.

Q.  You're not going to tell us that these flashing lights were not in D's eyes when you were performing the eye check?

A.  As I said, I don't believe they affected him.

Q.  Tell me, have you ever been to the eye doctor?

A.  Yes.

Q.  For an examination?

A.  Yes.

Q.  When the doctor was conducting the examination of your eyes, did he have red and blue strobe lights flashing in your eyes?

A.  No.

*Q.*  How about flashing halogen lights? Did he have these types of lights flashing about while conducting an examination of your eyes?

*A.*  No.

*Q.*  How about car headlights shining in your eyes during the examination?

*A.*  No.

*Q.*  Do you think that there might be a good reason why eye doctors do not have obnoxious and distracting colored lights flashing on and off during their eye examinations?

*A.*  [Who cares what his answer is.]

*Q.*  By the way, don't strobe lights tend to make smooth movements look choppy, like at a disco?

*A.*  They can.

*Q.*  And you were examining D's eyes under pretty similar conditions?

*A.*  As I said, I don't believe the flashing lights inferred with my evaluation.

## WALK AND TURN (WAT)

*Q.*  You also asked D to perform a Walk and Turn exercise?

*A.*  That's correct.

*Q.*  And you instructed him how to perform this exercise?

*A.*  Yes.

*Q.*  But as you said, you did not tell him what factors you were going to grade him on?

*A.*  No.

*Q.*  We spoke earlier about cars driving by while D was trying to do your exercises.

*A.*  Yes.

*Q.*  And we've already spoken about how these cars driving by at high speeds tend to create wind disturbances, correct?

*A.*  Yes.

*Q.*  I recall many instances in which my car was actually moved as a result of wind blasts created by passing cars and trucks. Has that ever happened to you?

*A.*  Yes.

*Q.*  You will agree that performing a balancing exercise can be difficult while cares are zooming by creating wind blasts that can actually move cars weighing over a ton?

*A.*  I don't recall if cars were actually driving by when D was doing the Walk and Turn.

*Q.*  Passing cars and trucks also tend to be distractions, don't they?

*A.*  I guess they could be.

*Q.*  Headlights and all?

*A.*  Yes.

*Q.*  And D performed this exercise on the road shoulder?

*A.*  Yes.

*Q.*  The shoulder off the highway?

*A.*  That's correct.

*Q.*  The shoulder that is not flat and level?

*A.*  Yes.

*Q.*  But there are no straight lines marked on the shoulder of the highway?

*A.*  I had him walk an imaginary straight line.

*Q.*  Not an actual line?

*A.*  No.

*Q.*  Not a visible line?

*A.*  No.

*Q.*  So this imaginary line that you saw in your head, D was supposed to figure out where that line was?

*A.*  Yes.

*Q.*  Now, could you please assume the starting position of this exercise?

*A.*  [Bullethead stands up, places heel to toes and keeps his hands by his sides.]

*Q.*  Is the posture you're in now a normal driving posture? In other words, is how you look now the way you look when you're behind the wheel of a car driving?

*A.*  No.

*Q.*  Exactly. Sitting in a comfortable car seat is completely different from walking heel to toe on a windblown highway with your arms by your sides, isn't it?

*A.*  I'm trying to test his ability to drive a car safely.

*Q.*  Driving is normal function that most people do with regularity, correct?

*A.*  Correct.

*Q.*  Walking with your heel against your toe and your arms down by your side, is that something that most people do with regularity?

*A.*  No.

*Q.*  Well, D did walk from his car over by your cruiser, right?

*A.*  Yes.

*Q.*  In your report, you don't mention anything about D stumbling or falling down, do you?

*A.*  No.

*Q.*  Then is it safe to assume that D did not stumble or fall down when given the opportunity to walk like an ordinary human?

*A.*  Yes.

*Q.* In fact, if you wanted to be fair to D, you could have had him walk — in a normal manner — up and down the whole highway shoulder to see if he was sure on his feet, couldn't you have?

*A.* I guess so.

*Q.* So in other words, on a dark night, with cars driving by, on a sloping highway shoulder not scattered with gravel and other debris, not knowing what he was being evaluated on, walking in an abnormal manner, and thinking that he could be arrested and thrown in jail, you claim that D did not follow the imaginary line you had in your mind and therefore he is drunk?

*A.* Yes.

*Q.* Instead of giving D negative points for each thing you say he did wrong, is it possible to give him positive points for things he does right?

*A.* I guess so. Yes.

*Q.* For instance, you said D stepped off your imaginary line twice, didn't he touch his heel with his toe three times, and made an improper turn. A total of six infractions. Is that correct?

*A.* Yes.

*Q.* So D didn't lose his balance during the instructions or start before being told to begin?

*A.* No. That's not how this test is graded.

*Q.* But if D had done either of those two things, you would have scored it against him as being proof that he was drunk.

*A.* That's the way I was taught to do it.

*Q.* As part of this exercise, you had D walk 18 steps: nine in one direction and then nine back. Correct?

*A.* Yes.

*Q.* And during each one of those 18 steps, D could have done something that you would have counted against him? Correct?

*A.* I don't know what you mean.

*Q.* Well, if D would have paused after his first step, would you have counted that as a point against D?

*A.* Yes. If the subject pauses once he starts walking, it is counted as a point tending to prove intoxication.

*Q.* Is it possible that D could have paused after each one of his 18 steps?

*A.* Yes.

*Q.* But he didn't.

*A.* No.

*Q.* Did you then score him 18 positive points as proof that he was not intoxicated?

*A.* No.

*Q.* But you could have?

*A.*  That's not the way I was trained.

*Q.*  You also required D to walk heel-to-toe for 18 steps. Correct?

*A.*  Yes.

*Q.*  And out of those 18 steps, his heel of one foot did not touch that of his other foot on three occasions?

*A.*  Correct.

*Q.*  That means on 15 occasions it was done perfectly?

*A.*  I guess so.

*Q.*  Did you give him 15 positive points showing he was not intoxicated?

*A.*  No.

*Q.*  And out of 18 chances to stepping on your imaginary line, D stepped off it twice?

*A.*  Yes.

*Q.*  That means on 16 occasions, it was done perfectly?

*A.*  Yes.

*Q.*  And of course, you didn't give him 16 positive points, did you?

*A.*  No.

*Q.*  If D would have raised his arms more than six inches from his side to balance himself while walking, you would have counted that as a point against him. Is that correct?

*A.*  Yes.

*Q.*  And he could have raised his arms during each of the 18 steps you required him to take. Correct?

*A.*  Yes.

*Q.*  But he didn't raise his arms, not even once?

*A.*  Yes.

*Q.*  And, of course, you didn't give him 18 positive points?

*A.*  No.

*Q.*  You say that D did, in your opinion, make an improper turn? Correct?

*A.*  Yes.

*Q.*  And there was only one turn that was required during this exercise?

*A.*  Yes.

*Q.*  And you did count this one improper turn against D?

*A.*  Yes.

*Q.*  You would also grade a point against D for taking the wrong number of steps. Is that correct?

*A.*  Yes.

*Q.*  But he walked the correct number of steps?

*A.*  Yes.

*Q.*  He walked 18 steps?

*A.*  Yes.

*Q.*  Did you give him 18 positive points?

*A.*  No.

*Q.*  Adding up all the negative points you give D, that totals 6 points. Is that correct? Two points off for stepping off your imaginary line, three points off for not touching heel-to-toe and one point off for making an improper turn. Correct?

*A.*  Yes.

*Q.*  Now let's add up all of D's positive points. One point for keeping his balance during instructions: One point for not starting too soon. Eighteen points for not stopping during the exercise; fifteen points for touching his heel-to-toe; sixteen points for walking dead straight on your imaginary line; 18 points for not using his arms for balancing; and eighteen points for taking the correct number of steps. That come out to a total of 87 positive points. Correct?

*A.*  That's not the way I compute the test.

*Q.*  Well I know that's not how you normally do it, but that's the way we're doing it here and now. Okay?

*A.*  Yes.

*Q.*  Now, D had 87 positive points and six negative points. That means D was being graded on 93 separate actions. Correct?

*A.*  I guess you could look at it that way.

*Q.*  With my calculator, could you please divide 87 by 93 [= 0.935]. When you get the answer, multiply it by 100 to put it in proper percentage form (= 93.5 percent). Please tell the jury what percent the number 87 is of 93?

*A.*  93.5 percent.

*Q.*  Isn't a scoring in the 90s generally considered an "A"?

*A.*  I guess so.

*Q.*  Have you ever failed a class in your life because you scored a 93.5 percent?

*A.*  No.

*Q.*  But even though D scored a 93.5 percent, he failed your test?

*A.*  Yes.


## ONE LEG STAND (OLS)

*Q.*  You also asked D to perform a One Leg Stand test?

*A.*  That's correct.

*Q.*  And you instructed him how to perform this exercise?

*A.*  Yes.

*Q.*  But as with the other exercises you had D perform, you did not tell him what factors you were going to grade him on?

*A.*  No.

*Q.*   We spoke earlier about cars driving by while D was trying to do your exercises?

*A.*   Yes.

*Q.*   Where do you think it's easier to balance yourself on one leg, on an uneven highway shoulder as cars go screaming by at high speeds at night with their headlights shining in your eyes, or in a police station?

*A.*   Easier.

*Q.*   Yes. Easier. Also fairer. Where would that be at?

*A.*   I guess at the police station.

*Q.*   Did you have D perform this exercise, or any other exercise, at the police station?

*A.*   No.

*Q.*   Could you have?

*A.*   I guess so.

*Q.*   So you only had him perform an exercise that he was totally unfamiliar with at a place, and under conditions, that you agree are not the most fair?

*A.*   Maybe.

*Q.*   Now, could you please assume the starting position of this exercise?

*A.*   [Bullethead stands up, places his hands by his sides, lifts one foot six inches off the ground and looks down at it.]

*Q.*   Is the posture you're in now a normal driving posture? In other words, is how you look now, the way you look when you're behind the wheel of a car driving?

*A.*   No.

*Q.*   Exactly. Again, sitting in a comfortable car seat is completely different from imitating a flamingo standing on one leg. Isn't it?

*A.*   I was trying to test his ability to drive a car safely.

*Q.*   Driving is a normal function that most people do with regularity, correct?

*A.*   Correct.

*Q.*   Balancing yourself on one leg with your arms down by your side, is that something that most people do with regularity?

*A.*   No.

*Q.*   Could you possible operate a car in the position you're in right now?

*A.*   Obviously, no.

*Q.*   In fact, there is not one driving skill that requires a person to balance himself in this awkward position?

*A.*   No.

*Q.*   But based on this unfamiliar, awkward, and unrelated-to-driving exercise that you had D perform, under unfair conditions, you claim that D was drunk?

A. That is my opinion.

Q. Well, let's count all the positive points that you could have given D, shall we?

A. Okay.

Q. For instance, you said that D put his foot down twice, and used his arms to maintain balance. Correct?

A. Yes.

Q. If you look through your report, you don't write down for how many seconds D was using his arms for balance, do you?

A. I really cannot recall exactly how long he used his hands for.

Q. But if D had used his arms for all 30 seconds of this exercise, that surely would have been significant enough for you to write that in your report, would it not?

A. I think so.

Q. And the same would hold true if he used him arms for 15 seconds — half the time. That definitely would have been significant enough for you to write that down, would it not?

A. I guess so.

Q. Well, the fact that you didn't write down how long he used his arms for balance, the amount of time that he used his arms to balance himself must have been relatively insignificant. As you said earlier, you were taught to write down all significant facts. Correct?

A. Yes.

Q. Let's go through your exercise, shall we?

A. Okay.

Q. To begin the exercise, D was required to stand at attention with his feet together and hands by his sides?

A. Yes.

Q. And he did that?

A. Yes, to start the exercise.

Q. Did you give him one positive point for correctly following your instructions?

A. No.

Q. But, again, you could have?

A. Yes.

Q. Now, this exercise required D to stand on one foot for a total of 30 seconds?

A. Yes.

Q. And you say D put his foot down twice. Correct?

A. Yes.

Q. That means that for 28 seconds, D performed this exercise correctly in this regard?

A. I guess so.

*Q.*  Did you score D 28 positive points?

*A.*  No.

*Q.*  There was nothing to prevent you from scoring D in this matter, is there?

*A.*  It's just not the way I was taught.

*Q.*  Under your standards, if D would have swayed at any time during the exercise, you would have graded that against D. Correct?

*A.*  Yes.

*Q.*  But you don't claim that D was swaying, do you?

*A.*  No. He wasn't swaying.

*Q.*  He wasn't swaying for all 30 seconds?

*A.*  Yes.

*Q.*  Well, did you give him 30 positive points for not swaying?

*A.*  No.

*Q.*  And as far as D using his arms for balancing, you will agree that because you left any mention of it out of your report, that he must have only used his arms for some small amount of time?

*A.*  I guess so.

*Q.*  We can only guess on this one, but let's give you the benefit of the doubt. D used his arms for about five seconds?

*A.*  Okay.

*Q.*  That leaves 25 positive points.

*A.*  Under the way that you are scoring him, yes.

*Q.*  If D would have hopped around during the exercise, that would have counted against him. Correct?

*A.*  Yes.

*Q.*  And he didn't hop around during this exercise?

*A.*  No.

*Q.*  Well, that's another 30 positive points in D's favor?

*A.*  Like I said, it's only in his favor the way you're scoring it.

*Q.*  And D also counted all the way to 30 before putting his foot down?

*A.*  Yes.

*Q.*  And D could have skipped numbers, or have mixed them up if he were drunk. Couldn't he?

*A.*  Yes.

*Q.*  But he didn't?

*A.*  No.

*Q.*  So let's give D another 30 positive points.

*A.*  That's not the way it's done.

*Q.*  Adding up all the negative points you gave D on this exercise, that totals seven points. Is that correct? Two points off for putting his foot down, and approximately five points off for using his hands. Correct?

*A.* Yes.

*Q.* Now let's add up all of D's positive points. One point for following your instructions regarding the positioning of his feet and hands; 28 points for keeping his foot in an unnatural position for so long; 30 points for being steady as a rock and not swaying; 25 points for balancing and not swaying; 30 points for being sure-footed and not hopping around; and another 30 points for having the mental faculties to count properly while under extremely difficult circumstances. That comes out to a total of 114 positive points. Correct?

*A.* That's not the way I compute the test.

*Q.* Well, I know that's not how you normally do it, but it's how we're doing it today. Okay?

*A.* Yes.

*Q.* Now, D had 114 positive points and seven negative points. That means D was being graded on 121 separate actions. Correct?

*A.* I guess you could look at it that way.

*Q.* With my calculator, could you please divide 114 by 121 [= 0.942]. When you get the answer, please multiply it by 100 to put it in proper percentage form [= 94.2 percent]. Please tell the jury what percent the number 114 is of 121?

*A.* 94.2 percent.

*Q.* Isn't scoring in the 90s generally considered getting an "A"?

*A.* I guess so.

*Q.* Have you ever failed a class in your life because you scored 94.2 percent?

*A.* No.

*Q.* But even though D scored a 94.2 percent, he failed your test?

*A.* Yes.


*Opportunity to Practice the SFST before "Grading"*

*Q.* You testified earlier that your opinion that D was drunk came from how he performed on the coordination and balance exercises, what you called "sobriety tests."

*A.* Yes, that's true.

*Q.* Is it your testimony that a person who is intoxicated cannot perform these exercises?

*A.* Yes.

*Q.* No matter how hard they try?

*A.* Yes.

*Q.* Well, after you told D what you wanted him to do, did you give him a chance to practice these exercises before you graded him?

*A.* No. That's not the way it's done.

Q. Yes. But you could have allowed D a practice run before you graded him?

A. I guess it could be done.

Q. And according to what you just said, no matter how many times you practice, it would not reflect the results?

A. I don't believe so.


*Politeness and Cooperation Proving Sobriety*

Q. You've testified that you told D that you wanted him to perform certain coordination and dexterity exercises?

A. Yes.

Q. Is there any law that says that D has to perform those exercises?

A. No, not that I know of.

Q. But D did agree to perform them?

A. Yes.

Q. So he was being cooperative. He wasn't one of those people that "stand on their rights." He agreed to perform these exercises, even though by law, he didn't have to?

A. Well, yes.

Q. Now, you have indicated to me that my client was being cooperative that evening?

A. Yes.

Q. And I assume that is because he complied with all of your orders and demands?

A. Yes.

Q. And he didn't give you any hassles?

A. No.

Q. Isn't it true that people who are impaired by alcohol are contentious and belligerent and difficult to deal with?

A. Well, a lot of the time. But not always.

Q. Well, as you just agreed with me, D was not any of those. He agreed to perform these difficult balancing and coordination exercises. Isn't being cooperative a mannerism that is more associated with a person who is sober, rather than drunk?

A. Yes, but not conclusively.

Q. But my client was perfect gentleman?

A. Well, yes.

Q. Now, can you turn to the jury and tell them why else my client was a perfect gentleman?

A. Blah, blah, blah.

Q. Now officer, you have also indicated that my client was polite?

A. Yes.

*Q.* And I assume that is because he said "yes sir" and "no sir."

*A.* Yes.

*Q.* And he spoke politely in other ways?

*A.* Yes.

*Q.* Could you turn and face and tell the jury what else you say my client did that was polite and respectful?

*A.* Blah, blah, blah.


*The Self-Comparison Issue*

*Q.* Now, you've testified earlier that you have never met D before the night you arrested him?

*A.* That's correct.

*Q.* Could you tell the jury how D normally responds to stressful situations?

*A.* I can only tell you what he was like on the night I arrested him.

*Q.* Is D a type of person who gets flustered easily?

*A.* I don't know.

*Q.* Does he normally get embarrassed easily?

*A.* I don't know.

*Q.* Do you normally know how he deals with these feelings?

*A.* I don't know.

*Q.* How smart is D?

*A.* I don't know.

*Q.* Is he normally a klutz?

*A.* I don't know.

*Q.* How about athletic ability? Is he generally athletic?

*A.* I don't know.

*Q.* So you have no idea how D would perform on your exercises if he had absolutely no alcohol in his body?

*A.* No.

*Q.* Wouldn't you agree that all people are different? They have different abilities?

*A.* Yes.

*Q.* Differences in strength?

*A.* Yes.

*Q.* Differences in muscle development?

*A.* Yes.

*Q.* Differences in their coordination?

*A.* Yes.

*Q.* Differences in their balancing abilities?

*A.* Yes.

*Q.* Differences in height?

A.  Yes.

Q.  Differences in weight?

A.  Yes.

Q.  Differences in the speed with which they learn new things?

A.  Yes.

Q.  Differences in their speech and manner of talking?

A.  Yes.

Q.  Differences in their memory ability?

A.  Yes.

Q.  Differences in their ability to learn and recall the instructions to strange and unusual exercises?

A.  Possibly.

Q.  Wouldn't you agree that people generally get better at performing exercises with more practice?

A.  Generally.

Q.  Do you know what my client's normal physical abilities are?

A.  No.

Q.  Do you know what his normal mental faculties are?

A.  No.

Q.  How about the judge's?

A.  No.

Q.  How about the prosecutor's?

A.  No.

Q.  How about juror # _____'s normal mental faculties?

A.  No.

Q.  How about any other member of the jury?

A.  No.

Q.  How about any other person in this courtroom, other than yourself?

A.  No.


*Conclusion*

Q.  Hypothetically speaking, if you pulled over some members of the jury on the highway, you smelled a strong odor of alcohol, you had them perform the same exercises you had D perform, and they performed them as well as D did, would you arrest them for drunk driving?

A.  Yes.

Q.  How about if they came back a day later with no alcohol in their bodies, and still couldn't perform your exercises. Would you still want them prosecuted for drunk driving?

A.  No.

Q.  Well, how about if you performed the same tests on some of the members of the jury, and they were completely sober — no alcohol whatsoever in their bodies — but they still performed your exercises as well as D, would you still arrest them for drunk driving?

A.  I'm not sure.

Q.  By the time you asked D to submit to a breath test back at the station, you already had D under arrest for being DUI, isn't that so?

A.  Yes.

Q.  And that was your opinion, that he was DUI?

A.  Yes.

Q.  Did you ever tell D that if he submitted to your breath test and tested under the legal limit, that you would unarrest him, apologize to him, and let him go?

A.  No.

Q.  And you made that quite clear to him by your actions and your words. He was under your arrest, and no matter what reading would have come out of your machine, he was going to remain under your arrest on DUI charges?

A.  Yes.

Q.  So he could have tested under the legal limit, but he was still going to remain under your arrest and have to go to trial, in front of this jury?

A.  Yes.

Q.  In fact, he could have tested .03 percent and he was still going to have to come to court and defend himself against you and your charges, isn't that true?

A.  Yes. [Attorney could then respond, "Then this machine that your department relies upon all the time to get drunk drivers off the road would have been wrong and you, of course, would have been right.]

A.  No. [Attorney could respond, "Then you are willing to concede that you do not trust your own judgment or your exercises; you are willing to defer to a machine to make your decision for you.]

Q.  Attorney: Nothing further.


## §13.3   *The Breath Operator and/or Blood-Alcohol Expert: Strategy and Techniques*


*Page 1002. Add after first full paragraph:*

Counsel should never overlook the potential value of the prosecution's blood-alcohol expert or laboratory technician for getting into evidence scientific articles relating to blood-alcohol analysis. Confronted with articles counsel has obtained that are favorable to the defense theory of the case, the witness must either confess ignorance or acknowledge his having either read it or being authored by a reliable authority in the field.

When the witness invariably testifies on direct examination as to his expert opinion concerning impairment, etc., keep in mind that most states permit him to be questioned concerning scientific literature in the field. California's Evidence Code §721(b) is a fairly typical example:

> If a witness testifying as an expert testifies in the form of an opinion, he or she may not be cross-examined in regard to the content or tenor of any scientific, technical, or professional text, treatise, journal, or similar publication unless any of the following occurs:
> (1) The witness referred to, considered, or relied upon such publication in arriving at or forming his or her opinion. . . .
> (3) The publication has been established as a reliable authority by the testimony or admission of the witness or by other expert testimony or by judicial notice.
> If admitted, relevant portions of the publication may be read into evidence but may not be received as exhibits.

A tactic used by the author with some success is to mail copies of relevant articles to the toxicologist/technician before trial, if he is known, and suggest that he read it — with the advisory that he will be asked about it on the stand. If he still claims not to have read the article(s), he can be presented to the jury as an "expert" who is uninterested in the literature of leading experts in his field.

## §13.4  Illustrative Cross-Examination of Operator/Expert

*Page 1050.  Add after end of material on "Blood Analysis":*

In a trial involving direct analysis of the blood, counsel should consider the following illustrative cross-examination of a law enforcement blood-alcohol expert by Charles J. Unger, of Glendale, California.*

Q. Good morning, Mr. Ting.
A. Good morning.
Q. Mr. Ting, you mentioned you have been with the sheriff's crime lab for the last six years; is that correct?
A. Yes.
Q. With respect to the blood alcohol section, you've been with that section for the last four years; is that right?
A. Yes.
Q. You mentioned you testified in court before, approximately 200 times; is that correct?
A. Yes.
Q. Would it be fair to say that all but a handful of those times you were called as an expert by the prosecution?
A. Yes.
Q. Mr. Ting, you mentioned you have your — you got your bachelor's degree in chemistry and biology at Irvine; is that correct?
A. Yes.
Q. That you're currently seeking your master's at Cal State, L.A.; correct?
A. Well, I've been enrolled in the program.
Q. In fact, you have been enrolled in that program for a considerable period of time, haven't you?
A. Yes.
Q. You enrolled in that program in 1981; is that correct?
A. That's correct.
Q. So for eight years you have been enrolled in the master's program; correct?
A. Yes.
Q. Mr. Ting, you indicated that — I think the quote was — you had had trouble with the gas chromatograph and you overcame it; is that correct?
A. Yes.
Q. The trouble occurred in February of 1986, didn't it?
A. Yes.
Q. And at that time your supervisor — you have a supervisor over at the crime lab, don't you?
A. Yes, I do.
Q. And his name is Dan Nathan?

*Reprinted with permission.

A.   Yes.

Q.   And in February of 1986 Mr. Nathan took you off the gas chromatograph because you couldn't get the duplicate analyses, the two analyses that you did, to agree with each other?

A.   That's correct.

Q.   And Mr. Nathan indicated to you at that time, did he not, that as soon as you discovered what you were doing wrong, what the problem was, that he would put you back on the gas chromatograph; correct?

A.   Yes.

Q.   Did you discover what you were doing wrong later in that month, in February?

A.   No.

Q.   March?

A.   No.

Q.   April?

A.   No.

Q.   It wasn't until August, was it?

A.   August, September.

Q.   Okay. Approximately six or seven months; correct?

A.   Yes.

Q.   And six or seven months later, you determined that you weren't sealing the vials tightly enough; is that correct?

A.   It wasn't tightly enough, it was properly. I was — after the sample is dispensed into the three-inch glass vial using the automatic dispenser, an aluminum cap is placed onto the vial and a vise grip is used to seal that cap around the vial. And I was not properly sealing the vials with the vise grip. I was not making a good airtight seal using the vise grip on the aluminum caps.

Q.   Mr. Ting, back in September, then, of 1986, Mr. Nathan let you go back to the gas chromatograph; correct?

A.   Yes.

Q.   With respect to your lab and their use of the gas chromatograph, you are allowed to run up to 45 samples per run, aren't you?

A.   Yes.

Q.   In fact, I think you indicated you did 43 in this case; is that correct?

A.   Forty-three on that particular date, 4/13/89. Yes.

Q.   Okay, thank you. Your laboratory permits the run to count if there are fewer than seven errors on the run; correct?

A.   Well, fewer than seven what are called "rejects," and rejects being the duplicate analyses differing from one another from the same blood sample by greater than plus or minus 5 percent of the average of the two results.

*Q.* So in other words, if 39 out of 45 agree with each other, the run will count and those 39 that agree will be used, and six that don't agree will be tossed or thrown out or not used or rerun; is that correct?

*A.* Well, the six to seven that do not agree would then be rerun.

*Q.* Okay, and if in fact 38 of them do agree within the plus or minus 5 percent and there are seven rejects, then the whole run is scrapped; correct?

*A.* Yes.

*Q.* But if there are 39 that would get through without a little "R" to show you — to indicate a reject —

*A.* Yes, a little "R" shows up on the computer-generated summary sheet on the right-hand side — far right-hand margin of the sheet.

*Q.* All right, if you get six out of every 45 rejects, the other 39 are permitted to remain and count — that's not a good word — are permitted to remain and the remainder of the run counts; correct?

*A.* Yes.

*Q.* And is there anything different done in your analysis of the 39 where you didn't get an "R" as opposed to the six where you did get an "R" to indicate a reject?

*A.* Generally, the cause of rejects are in the — are due to the improper sealing of the blood vials — or the three-inch glass vials with the aluminum caps.

*Q.* But the laboratory does not require you to reanalyze those other 39 that are going to count and be considered valid; is that correct?

*A.* That's correct.

*Q.* Mr. Ting, I take it — or I think you indicated you base part of your expertise on the knowledge of the literature; is that correct?

*A.* Yes.

*Q.* Mr. Ting, are you familiar with an article by Dr. Sheldon Plotkin entitled "Most Direct Blood Testing for Alcohol Content Is in Error"?

*A.* No, I'm not.

*Q.* All right, do you know the rules — I can only question you about articles that you have read and relied upon.

　　Mr. Ting, have you read and relied upon an article by Dr. Sidney Kay entitled "The Collection and Handling of the Blood Alcohol Specimen?"

*A.* No.

*Q.* Mr. Ting, have you read and relied upon an article entitled "The Stability of Ordinary Blood-Alcohol Samples Held for Various Periods of Time Under Different Conditions" by Drs. Glenn, Denning, and Waugh?

A.  I don't believe so.

Q.  How about one entitled "Determination of Fluoride in Blood Samples for Analysis of Alcohol" by N. K. Shajani?

A.  I don't believe so.

Q.  And lastly, "Effects and Mechanisms of Sodium Fluoride in Forensic Alcohol Samples" by Heude, John Heude?

A.  I don't believe so.

Q.  Well, then let me ask it a different way: What have you read and relied on that pertains to blood-alcohol testing specifically?

A.  Specifically, I've read approximately 20 to 25 articles with respect to the proper preservation and handling of blood samples. And probably an additional maybe 50 to 100 other articles pertaining directly with the analysis of samples with respect to blood-alcohol determinations.

Q.  All right, with respect to blood tests specifically, can you give me the name of a couple of articles that you've read, please.

A.  Not by — not by title alone, no.

Q.  Can you give me perhaps one title of something you've read pertaining to blood alcohol tests?

A.  Well, one of the most extensive articles I've read covers almost all aspects of alcohol, alcohol and driving and also alcohol and the impaired driver.

Q.  That's put out by the American Medical Association; correct?

A.  Yes.

Q.  I'm talking about articles specifically that go to blood testing as opposed to more generalized articles that talk about alcohol and the effects on the human body.

A.  By title alone, I could not give you a title alone.

Q.  Mr. Ting, fermentation is a process by which sugar converts into alcohol; correct?

A.  Yes.

Q.  Sugar is present in the blood of all humans; is that right?

A.  Yes.

Q.  The vials that are used in these type of cases are supposed to have a certain amount of preservative in them, aren't they, to prevent fermentation?

A.  Yes.

Q.  They are also supposed to have a certain amount of anticoagulant in them to prevent coagulating; correct?

A.  Yes.

Q.  The preservative used in these types of vials is called sodium fluoride; is that correct?

A.  Yes.

*Q.* At any time — well, does your laboratory prepare the vials itself? Does it put the preservative or anticoagulant in it?

*A.* No, it does not.

*Q.* In fact, the laboratory orders these vials en masse from a company called Terumo; is that correct?

*A.* Yes.

*Q.* And your laboratory — your laboratory orders these vials several thousand at a time; is that correct?

*A.* Probably.

*Q.* All right. And when your laboratory gets these vials in, are any of them tested at that time to determine whether or not there's a proper amount of preservative in the vials?

*A.* Not to my knowledge.

*Q.* Well, how about when you analyze the vial for blood-alcohol content, do you test it for preservative level at that time?

*A.* No.

*Q.* A proper amount of preservative is in fact necessary to flow or prevent fermentation; correct?

*A.* Yes.

*Q.* Mr. Ting, the literature also indicates that refrigeration is important with respect to fermentation, doesn't it?

*A.* Well, refrigeration is one way to ensure proper preservation of a blood sample, and the addition of a sufficient amount of preservative would be another.

*Q.* All right, now, you analyzed this blood nine days after it was drawn, correct?

*A.* That I don't know.

*Q.* All right. Do you have your slip up there with you, Mr. Ting?

*A.* I have a Xerox copy of the laboratory receipt and also the computer-generated summary sheet, which indicates the day I would have analyzed the sample.

*Q.* All right, this is what I'm looking for. May I?

*A.* Sure.

*Q.* Thank you. Mr. Ting, this indicates an analysis date of April thirteenth, correct?

*A.* Yes.

*Q.* Now, this April fifth date, does that indicate that that's the day when your lab received this blood?

*A.* No, actually April sixth, the date headed by the box. The date on the laboratory receipt being 4/6/89.

*Q.* All right. So you — this blood basically sat in the laboratory from 4/6/89 until you analyzed it on 4/13/89; correct?

*A.* Well, actually, it sat a little longer. Because it was not until 4/19/89 that I returned the sample to the evidence control section or evidence locker at the crime lab.

*Q.* All right, I'm talking about the time it sat before you analyzed it would be from 4/6 to 4/13?

*A.* In the crime lab, yes.

*Q.* All right. In the crime lab you don't refrigerate the vials, do you?

*A.* No, we do not.

*Q.* All right. So assuming that the evidence was first placed in an unrefrigerated locker at Whittier P. D. and then put in your crime lab refrigerator, we have a nine-day period of unrefrigerated blood from the time the blood was drawn to the time it was analyzed; is that correct?

*A.* I don't know what date the sample was drawn.

*Q.* Mr. Ting, in your reading, in your reliance upon the literature, is time important as far as the time from when the sample was drawn to when in fact you do your analysis?

*A.* Not really, if the sample is properly preserved.

*Q.* Okay, that's really what it comes down to, isn't it, whether the sample was properly preserved?

*A.* Yes.

*Q.* Mr. Ting, police officers, well, they don't have an opportunity themselves to measure preservative, but they can look inside a vial and see if there is at least something in there, can't they?

*A.* Yes.

*Q.* Well, assuming that there's something in there of an unknown quantity, what would a police officer expect to see?

*A.* A powder inside of the vial — unused blood vial.

*Q.* And what color would that powder be?

*A.* That depends. The older blood vials, the preservative and anticoagulant used to appear as a white powder. As of about 1986, the vials since 1986 purchased by the sheriff's crime lab, the preservative and anticoagulant appears as a light pink, light purple color.

*Q.* So then basically for the last four years, if an officer were to see what is in fact preservative and anticoagulant, he would look in and see something pink or purple in color?

*A.* Depending whether or not a new blood vial versus an old blood vial are used.

*Q.* Are blood vials ordered from 1985 still being used?

*A.* Occasionally.

*Q.* That would be a four-year-old vial?

*A.* Yes.

*Q.*  Would it be fair to say that 90 percent of the time or so new vials are in fact used?

*A.*  Well, I don't know of an exact number, but the vast majority of the vials submitted to the crime lab currently would be the newest blood vials. Every now and then, occasionally, a very old blood vial is submitted to the crime lab.

*Q.*  All right, when you say every now and then, I take it that would be a rare or unusual occurrence; is that correct?

*A.*  I would say a rare occurrence.

*Q.*  All right. Mr. Ting, when you analyzed the blood, you analyzed a quarter of a milliliter; is that correct?

*A.*  The automatic dispenser places into each three-inch glass vial a quarter of a milliliter of blood so that is then done in duplicate. So at least a half milliliter of blood is removed from the blood vial, the original blood vial, when the sample is collected from the subject.

*Q.*  All right. So you're analyzing a quarter, two different times, to equal a half then; correct?

*A.*  Yes.

*Mr. Unger.*  All right, thank you. Thank you. I have nothing further.

*The Court.*  Redirect.


## REDIRECT EXAMINATION

*By Ms. Felix.*

*Q.*  You testified that earlier in your training you had some difficulties. Now, you are now working on the gas chromatograph at the sheriff's lab; is that correct?

*A.*  Yes.

*Q.*  Who is your supervisor there?

*A.*  Mr. Dan Nathan.

*Q.*  Is that the same Mr. Dan Nathan that defense counsel referred to as having taken you off from doing work on the gas chromatograph back in 1986?

*A.*  Yes.

*Q.*  Thank you. Are you familiar with Title 17 of the California Code—?

*A.*  Yes.

*Q.*  — in reference to refrigeration of blood samples?

*A.*  I don't believe Title 17 directly addresses refrigeration. Title 17 requires that samples be properly preserved. I don't believe it necessarily states that there is a need to refrigerate samples.

*Q.*  Thank you. Now when you went to do your tests on the vial that you received around nine days after the blood sample was supposed to have been taken, was the blood coagulated?

*A.*   I have no indication of such.

*Q.*   Based on your training and experience in biology and blood analysis, would you have been able to see if the blood had been coagulated?

*A.*   With the exception of very, very small minute clots, because generally blood clots are big enough to be seen by the naked eye.

*Q.*   Now, the run you did — the runs you did on April thirteenth, 1989, which you show on the calibration sheet there, was that an acceptable run?

*A.*   Yes, it was.

*Q.*   So would you say that in your opinion when you received that vial of blood on October — or April thirteenth, 1989, to begin doing a blood-alcohol analysis, there was no coagulation that you could determine? The evidence envelope was intact, you had no difficulty doing the analysis using the gas chromatograph, and the gas chromatograph was in proper working order; is that correct?

*A.*   Yes.

*Q.*   Has anything the defense questioned you about where you've given your answer about — change your opinion of what a person with a blood-alcohol level of .14 would be considered as under the influence, in your opinion?

*A.*   No.

*Ms. Felix.*   Nothing further, Your Honor.

*The Court.*   Mr. Unger.

*Mr. Unger.*   Thank you, Your Honor.


**RECROSS-EXAMINATION**

*By Mr. Unger.*

*Q.*   Mr. Ting, we have no quarrel with the .14. In fact, it is your opinion, just to make sure that's clear, that all people at .10 or above are under the influence of alcohol for purposes of driving, you'd agree with that, wouldn't you?

*A.*   Yes.

*Q.*   All right. Mr. Ting, you answered counsel's questions with respect to whether you saw any — anything occurring with respect to coagulant. My question to you would be, at no time did you or anyone with your lab, either when the vials came in or when you analyzed it for alcohol content, test the vial to determine how much, if any, preservative was in it, did you?

*A.*   To the best of my knowledge, that's correct.

*Q.*   All right. Mr. Ting, Title 17, which was referred to by counsel, gives a list of steps with respect to how blood is supposed to be drawn by a nurse or a lab technician, doesn't it?

A.   Nurse, lab technician or other qualified personnel drawing blood samples, yes.

Q.   All right, it talks about blood samples by venepuncture?

A.   Yes.

Q.   It also indicated that alcohol or other volatile organic disinfectants should not be used to clean the skin where a specimen is to be drawn, correct?

A.   Yes.

Q.   It also indicates that blood samples should be collected using sterile, dry hypodermic needles and syringes?

A.   Yes.

Q.   It basically gives a road map on how the nurse or lab technician or qualified individual should draw the blood; correct?

A.   Yes.

Q.   These procedures are the law in this state, aren't they?

A.   Yes.

*Mr. Unger.*   Thank you. I have nothing further.

*The Court.*   Ms. Felix.


## FURTHER REDIRECT EXAMINATION

*By Ms. Felix.*

Q.   Do you have anything or has anything been indicated to you that the blood was not properly drawn in this case?

A.   No.

Q.   When you did your analysis on the blood, was there anything in there that would indicate to you that possibly the blood may have been drawn incorrectly?

A.   Not that I was aware of.

*Ms. Felix.*   Thank you. Nothing further, Your Honor.

*The Court.*   Anything else, Mr. Unger?

*Mr. Unger.*   Briefly, Your Honor.


## FURTHER RECROSS-EXAMINATION

*By Mr. Unger.*

Q.   Mr. Ting, you don't know anything about how the blood was drawn in this case, do you?

A.   No.

*Q.*  And in fact if there were problems, you wouldn't necessarily expect to see something in the vial, would you? I mean, it is possible that you would. But you wouldn't necessarily expect to, would you?

*A.*  If for instance, an improper swabbing agent had been used to cleanse the arm, I would not be able to see that in the blood sample itself. So in that regard, yes.

*Q.*  All right. And if fermentation or some sort of degeneration had occurred, that's not something you would visually be able to determine whether or not it had occurred, correct?

*A.*  Right, that's something you cannot see.

*Mr. Unger.*   Thank you very much. Nothing further.

*The Court.*   Ms. Felix?

*Ms. Felix.*   Nothing further, Your Honor.

*The Court.*   May Mr. Ting be excused, Counsel?

*Mr. Unger.*   Yes, Your Honor.

*The Court.*   Ms. Felix, may Mr. Ting be excused?

*Ms. Felix.*   Yes, Your Honor.

*The Court.*   Thank you, Mr. Ting.

*The Witness.*   Thank you.

# RESOURCES

*Expert witnesses*

*Page 1146. Note the following correction:*

Dr. Richard Jensen's telephone number has been changed to (651–784–7721) (fax: 651–784–7250).

# BIBLIOGRAPHY

*Books and Pamphlets*

Whited & Nichols, Drinking/Driving Litigation Criminal and Civil (2d ed.)

*Articles*

Bode, et al., Effects of Cimetidine Treatment on Ethanol Formation in the Human Stomach, 19(6) Scandinavian Journal of Gastroenterology 853 (1984)

Ericson, Effects of Antacids on Alcohol's Reaction, 5(5) Alcoholism 28 (1985)

Jones & Neri, 24 Canadian Society of Forensic Sciences Journal 165 (1991)

Labianca, D.A., How Specific for Ethanol Is Breath-Alchol Analysis Based on Absorption of IR Radiation at 9.5 microns?, 16 Journal of Analytical Toxicology 404 (1992)

Labianca & Simpson, Medicolegal Alcohol Determination: Variability of the Blood- to Breath-Alcohol Ratio and Its Effect on Reported Breath-Alcohol Concentrations, 33 European Journal of Clinical Chemistry 919 (1995)

Moskowitz, Burns & Ferguson, Police Officers' Detection of Breath Odors from Alcohol Ingestion, 31(3) Accident Analysis and Prevention 175 (May 1999)

Saunders, News of Science, Medicine and Technology: Straight Talk, 21(10) Discover (Oct. 2000)

Simpson, The New "Direct Breath" Statutes: Both Bad Law and Bad Science, 6(4) DWI Journal 1 (1991)

# TABLE OF CASES

# INDEX

# DRUNK DRIVING DEFENSE
2001 Cumulative Supplement

*This supplement supersedes all previous supplements.*